Ideas Generation

For Nevenko Eddie Herceg
1932–1998
The best ideas generator of them all

Ideas Generation

Tools for being constantly fresh, creative and original

ROSEMARY HERCEG & TIM FLATTERY

Published in Australia by
New Holland Publishers (Australia) Pty Ltd
Sydney • Auckland • London • Cape Town

14 Aquatic Drive Frenchs Forest NSW 2086 Australia
218 Lake Road Northcote Auckland New Zealand
86 Edgware Road London W2 2EA United Kingdom
80 McKenzie Street Cape Town 8001 South Africa

First published in 2000 by Lansdowne Publishing Pty Ltd
This edition published in 2000 by New Holland
Publishers (Australia) Pty Ltd

Copyright © 2000 in text: Pophouse Pty Ltd

All rights reserved. No part of this publication may be reproduced, stored in a retrieval system or transmitted, in any form or by any means, electronic, mechanical, photocopying, recording or otherwise, without the prior written permission of the publishers and copyright holders.

National Library of Australia Cataloguing-in-Publication Data:

Herceg, Rosemary.
Ideas generation : tools for being constantly fresh, creative and original.

ISBN 1 86436 705 9.

1. Thought and thinking. 2 . Creative thinking.
3. Problem solving. I. Flattery, Tim. II. Title.

153.42

Concepts and techniques developed at Pophouse in 1997 and tested in the field 1997–2000.

Designer: Mark Thacker, Big Cat Design
Printer: McPherson's Printing Group, Australia

This book is set in Garamond and Meta on Quark XPress

Foreword

Most people rarely think of themselves as ideas generators. Most people also think they are incapable of creativity and originality.

This book is about proving exactly the opposite. Creativity is a natural human trait. No one is more creative than the next person. There is no magic formula to being creative – because we are all born with an abundance of ideas within us, just waiting to come out. No one has cornered the market on creativity. Accountants are as creative as artists.

We are in the midst of the most exciting era to date – the ideas era. This era will be more exciting than any that has come before. It will make the Industrial Revolution seem like a blip on the radar. It will also give many of us the chance to do something we have always wanted to do: come up with great ideas and sell them to the world.

We have written *Ideas Generation* to inspire everyone who has ever had an idea to do something about it. We've all had at least one great idea and done absolutely nothing to see it through to the end. We've developed a process to help you access these ideas.

The Pophouse 21 step process is called S.I.m.P.L.e – the 21 Step Ideas Production Line. Throughout the three years of our company history, we have used this process to generate ideas for our clients and for ourselves as well. As a company that develops original strategies for other companies to capitalise on the New Economy, we need to remain constantly creative.

The one universal truth about ideas is that the most resilient person wins. We hope that you remember this as

ideas generation

you develop your own ideas. Ideas generation should be fun, it should inspire, it should give you a way to get the ideas out of your system. It should also constantly remind you to never be precious about your ideas: to let them go if they aren't very good and to explore them when they are great.

Above all, ideas generation is about the law of averages. You need one hundred ideas to have one great one. There is rarely such a thing as an overnight success and getting an idea out of your head and into the market will take a long time and be a long and winding road. But the rewards are enormous and the world is always ready for another great idea.

Have a great time ideas generating!

Rosemary Herceg   Tim Flattery
CEO Pophouse   Creative Director Pophouse

CONTENTS

1 **An introduction to ideas**   9
General overview to ideas in the 21st century.

2 **Why ideas are like cancer and how to control them**   25
A look at managing the ideas process for both business and personal use.

3 **Breaking the rules**   49
How to overcome the obstacles the world puts in your way.

4 **Thinking the unthinkable**   59
Tips for keeping your brain in tip-top condition and keeping it thinking originally.

5 **Incorporating consumer trends into the ideas process**   95
How trends can help you develop timely ideas.

6 **The 21 Step Ideas Production Line: S.l.m.P.L.e. Steps 1 to 7**   119
Generating thousands of ideas for yourself, your business and your future.
Doubling your failure rate. Avoiding linear thought by making unexpected connections. Creating a context for divergent thinking.

7   **Steps 8 to 14**   151
    How to spot the great ideas from the not-so-great.
    Grading and storing ideas.
    Simmering ideas slowly, cooking them gently.
    Incubating your ideas. Techniques for maintaining
    perspective. Investigating and editing ideas.

8   **Steps 15 to 21**   173
    Selling your ideas. Techniques for being heard.
    How to best illustrate your ideas. Defining a market
    for your ideas.

9   **Using the Internet as an ideas tool**   193
    Online research and marketing resources.

10 **Basic protection for your ideas**   229
    What are your intellectual property rights and
    how can you protect your ideas?

11 **The road ahead**   265
    A final thought. Five things to remember.

1

An introduction to ideas

General overview to ideas in the 21st century.

Ideas. The ideas millennium. Ideas people. Where do ideas come from? How can you train your mind to come up with more and more ideas that actually work? What can you do to make sure you always have the best ideas out of anyone in the room, anyone in your class, anyone in your company or corporation? How can your ideas make you incredibly wealthy?

These questions are consuming thousands of corporations and people alike as we open the door on a new millennium, a new era of humanity and a new business age. In fact success in the future may well depend on your ability to continually generate new ideas.

No one can genuinely claim to predict the future, but as we look forward into the new millennium two things become abundantly clear: *One,* we are all currently living through some of the largest economic and social changes

ideas generation

ever experienced by human beings. And *two*, you will not have a better opportunity to exercise your own creativity in your lifetime than right now!

Make no mistake: we are in the midst of a great gold rush, the likes of which we haven't witnessed in a hundred years. Remember the images of horses and cowboys as they rode madly toward El Dorado and the goldfields in the American wild west? Well it's happening again, except this time: *ideas are the gold of the 21st century*. El Dorado is not a place but a state of mind. Examples of recent discoveries fill the newspapers each day (like the story of a middle-aged couple who recently floated their Internet idea for $75 million). Just think, any one of the thousands of people dreaming up schemes on the Internet right now could unearth a multi-million-dollar idea this week. Why shouldn't it be you? Now is definitely the time to fossick around your brain for that one golden idea that could transform your career, your corporation and your life.

That's where we come in. Reading this book will take you a long way to harnessing your true creative potential. You will learn the key techniques we have used to turn some of Australia's leading corporations into 'ideas companies', and discover how to apply them to your own personal circumstances.

We have four simple goals in writing this book:
1. To help you better understand how your ideas are generated.
2. To explain how you can dramatically increase the volume and value of ideas that you generate.
3. To provide you with genuine techniques that help you spot a great idea from an average idea. And...
4. To share some insights on how best to get ideas sold and 'off the ground'.

1 An introduction to ideas

If you have bought this book, more than likely you already believe yourself to be an 'ideas person' – capable of imaginative and original thinking. In our opinion, everyone is an 'ideas person' in a way. Human history is littered with great ideas, from the pyramids to drive-through eating. But that certainly doesn't explain why some people continually get their ideas off the ground and others regularly fail to do so. How many times have you seen someone make millions from an idea that you had two years ago? How many times have you seen something and said to yourself, "I could have thought of that!" Don't worry, it happens to everyone, partly because we all share common experiences, partly because if you have an idea someone else in the world is usually not far behind you. The difference is that the people who are successful know how to turn their ideas into reality.

We have given a good deal of space to explaining some of the key differences between successful ideas people and the not-so-successful ones. This book is designed to be an *ideas toolbox* that you can constantly refer to at any time. It has deliberately been written in an easily accessible format to allow for a more holistic explanation of the techniques and concepts we explore. The concepts in *Ideas Generation* are not exclusively designed for people who want to float a $75 million idea, either. Many of our techniques are just as useful around the home or at your school as they are for a multi-national corporation. No matter what your final application, there is one thing that all readers will have in common: *The ultimate deciding factor in your success will be your own level of commitment to evolving your mind into a true creative force.* And you will see how to put your ideas into action.

ideas generation

We know enough about ideas people to know that you are an impatient lot and at this point you may be starting to feel the desire to jump ahead. No short cuts will actually help you, but if you are a 'Type A' person who looks at the answers to crossword puzzles we understand that you will need some sort of magic formula right now to keep you reading. Well, here it is: *Imagination + Discipline = Great Ideas.* People like George Lucas, creator of Star Wars, seem to live by this formula. You will notice that like all good equations it is a great example of balance, imagination being the free-form or 'loose' component and discipline the short form or 'tight' component. Many of our concepts are built on a 'loose/tight' equation for a very good reason. That said, for those of you who have evolved out of the 'Type A' mentality and would like to know more, read on.

Our techniques for improving the *volume and value* of your ideas are simple and obvious (you will also discover that simplicity is one of the most basic tests of a good idea) and they are lessons that do not require hours of application. But we will issue one warning: These techniques challenge the rules. They will also challenge the way you are used to thinking about how the world works. We will go so far as to say that you should approach the thinking and concepts in this book with a completely clean mental slate if you can.

If you find it difficult to visualise a clean mental slate, try this technique that works for us: From now on ...

assume everything you know is wrong,

or if you prefer ...

assume you know nothing.

Imagine an extraterrestrial life form dropping in for Sunday lunch and quietly explaining that *everything you have learned is a well-constructed figment of the collective human imagination.* The five-day working week, mortgages, CNN News, bosses, governments, taxes, even the twenty-four-hour day – all have been invented by people over the last 5000 years to satisfy a human need for structure in an unstructured universe. Only life, death, night, day and the four seasons are set in stone. If you need even more help visualising the concept we suggest you see the film *The Matrix*, which plays with this idea.

Really think about this concept for a while...

Liberating isn't it!

This whole exercise is designed to illustrate the fact that many obstacles you perceive in the way of your idea are just as much figments of your imagination as the idea itself. In fact, all obstacles are just someone's idea brought to life.

Generating great ideas is thankfully not yet a science. Big corporations and governments have yet to work out how to create a computer program that can do what comes naturally to millions of people. They seem to be trying though. (A very big software firm, wanting to create a basic computer program using the techniques in this book, approached us very recently.) Government and big business have however, worked out many ways of making millions of people doubt their own creative abilities. (This is a very important point; you should take some time to reflect on some recent examples where you have been forced into doubting yourself.) They usually do this by ensuring that all the employees' ideas automatically belong to the company and also by ensuring that actually getting an idea off the ground costs hundreds of thousands of dollars – both of which deal the individual *out* and the company *in*.

ideas generation

In Australia, where there are no genuine tax incentives to entice the creation of a venture capital culture, the obstacles facing ideas people are even greater. This is a critical point, and one that needs the urgent attention of the regulators in Canberra. Think about people in other parts of the world for a moment. If you are lucky enough to live in the US and you have an idea for a new Internet product, for example, thousands of venture capitalists are prepared to give you millions of speculative dollars based on the idea alone. In the US, money is handed over on business plans alone – with clear exit strategies for venture capitalists. Very different from the Australian experience!

It's a serious point, considering that the future prosperity of Australia could now well be in the hands of ideas people. If Australia is to truly compete in the new e-commercial, all-digital global economy, then it is imperative that we create a fertile environment for the generation, development, funding and export of ideas. In our work with the Australia Council for the Arts we gave this concept a catchphrase: *IDEAS SHOULD BE AUSTRALIA'S 21ST CENTURY 'SHEEP'S BACK'*. Great ideas will not only be the financial foundation for your own personal wealth in the new century, they can also solve a large part of Australia's balance of payments problem. If you doubt this, consider what America exports to the world. Mostly they export ideas. In fact, a staggering 42 per cent of US exports are ideas in the form of movies, music, software, books and a plethora of other examples of intellectual capital. Food for thought.

If the techniques in this book do no more than raise the awareness of the great opportunities there are for people (and countries) with great ideas, we will have achieved some of our goals. Make no mistake. We are all

1 An introduction to ideas

blessed to live in an age where we can make an extraordinarily good living by generating great and original ideas. The Internet generation is the luckiest ever. You'd better believe it – we're living right in the middle of the 'good old days'. Right now is the golden era of humanity and this book will open some of the many doors to help you take advantage of the ideas millennium.

But can intuition, creativity and imagination really be taught? This is a valid question, one we are asked by every one of our clients, and the answer is the same for the individual as for the corporation: *The ability to create great ideas can definitely be taught.* In fact it is probably more important to unlearn some of the habits you have picked up on your way through school, university and the workforce. What you especially *need* to learn is how to make your good ideas great and more importantly, how to identify a surefire winner. The techniques in this book will help demystify the whole process. In later chapters you will see we have created 21 steps that act as a *mental production line* for your ideas. Of course, rejects will come off your production line and there will be factory seconds, too. But most importantly, our *21 Step Ideas Production Line* will help you produce volumes of ideas that can be graded in terms of their quality, viability and value.

These techniques work. As we have already discussed, there is no true scientific basis for them, so they are based on success in the real world. The *21 Step Ideas Production Line* or (as we like to call it) 'S.I.m.P.L.e.' for short, has enabled us to sell ideas to individuals and companies, and this is why we have written this book.

We also have road tested our techniques over the last three years in one of the most cut-throat businesses in the world – marketing, an industry that creates demand for products for which, before marketing, people didn't know they had a need. Our company, Pophouse, which was a little idea we created out of nothing in 1996 and put into action with $1000, is now a little big company that feeds ideas into some of the biggest companies in the world. Seven days a week, fifty-two weeks a year we look at the world around us, at what people may like to do, to enjoy more of in the near future and we give birth to ideas. Lots of them. In any one working day we will come up with more than twenty-five ideas (based on a watertight rationale) that are either 'stockpiled' in our 'ideas inventory' or sold on to companies and institutions in Australia and the U.S. One of our biggest expenses is constantly trademarking concepts, designs, phrases and ideas. We will deal with the protection of your ideas in a later chapter.

Our best ideas are kept in a safe in one of the country's biggest banks. We admit that this is a little dramatic, but if you don't value your ideas as a first step, how is anyone else going to place a value on them? The not-so-good ones go into a holding pattern on our Web server where we can access and nurture them further. Knowing which ones to trash and not pursue is the real genius!

We think up ideas for a living. That's not hard: it's fun and it's easy and anyone can do it. What we have found more difficult is timing. More often than not an idea won't be bad but its *timing* will be wrong. Picking the right time to express your ideas in a day or indeed the right time in a conversation is crucial. Understanding your audience is so hard and requires so much work and intuition that many people let themselves and their ideas down right there. On the other hand, you also need to know when to ignore everyone and move pigheadedly forward until you achieve your goal. Sometimes when people tell you you're crazy you know you are on to a good thing.

The ideas business is also a volume business. To be a genuine force, an ideas company should have more than 2000 ideas in its inventory. All companies should take a formal approach to ideas management. Nor should they limit their scope of ideas to one field or one category. For example, we have found many accountants to be some of the most creative and original thinkers we have met (and we are certainly not referring to creative accounting!). An individual should also aim to generate at least ten good ideas a month. Ideas should be kept like exotic plants. You can't just leave them be; they need to be watered and checked on every once in a while. You should bring them out into the sun on occasion and see if they are still flourishing: because they are precious, you should care for them.

Imagine having a room in your house devoted to ideas. We saw one such house where the rumpus room was converted into an ideas room. The walls were covered with pieces of paper with all sorts of ideas written on them. The whole family used this room on a regular basis and each family member helped the others with the different ideas that obsessed them. To express their ideas, all the children had to do was to pick up the digital video camera and speak into it. The parents of these kids claimed that they had three full videotapes of their children's ideas. What a wonderful record of their children's imaginations, if nothing else! And what a wonderful way to train the kids in the power of ideas. Have you ever seen a child express an idea? It's one of the most inspiring things in the world. Children seem to generate hundreds of ideas all the time. This book will, we hope, make you feel childish in a good way. You see, ideas are often innocent and naïve. They bring out the child in us. Your eyes should sparkle when an idea 'hits' you.

But ideas are now much more than child's play. Ideas and the ability to constantly come up with them will be one of the most highly prized skills in the new century. A large part of our business also involves advising corporations on how the world will change in the future. They also tell us about the kinds of people they will wish to employ in the new millennium. Right now they are telling us that there is a severe shortage of 'original thinkers' and people who have great business sense as well as great ideas. Some of the world's most high-profile companies are even considering implementing ideas departments throughout their various business units, where teams of ideas directors will be the custodians of the corporate ideas inventory. When you think of it this way, you finally understand what lawyers mean by 'intellectual capital'. Ideas could well appear on the positive side of balance sheets in the future.

But what do we truly know about ideas? There is no scientific analysis of the function the brain plays in creating ideas. You can't exactly go to university to get a master's degree in Ideas either. So how can people harness their creativity and their ability to always be original? What can we learn from studying the common personality traits shared by history's greatest thinkers?

We have found that original thought can be taught; original thinkers can be trained. Like many other functions of the brain better documented in detail, the ability to think creatively has as much to do with process as it has to do with talent. When parents tell a child they are gifted or they have great natural talent in a certain area from an early age, they are giving the child permission to excel. But we are more likely to tell ourselves and other people the thousands of reasons why we won't succeed. We spend countless hours creating boundaries and limitations for our lives so that we do not experience disappointment. It is a simple and understandable defence mechanism.

Mathematics is a great example. We recently had a client who employed us to help her retrain her ability to think creatively. As we were discussing the various aspects to her character that were important, she told us that she had been a gifted mathematician from a very early age (no great surprise; she was a well known American stockbroker). It was no great surprise either to learn that her parents had encouraged her all the way in her academic pursuits – giving her permission to be a great mathematician in the process. This is not intended to be a book about personal success and giving yourself permission to succeed, but the point is an important one.

But we don't all grow up in an environment where we are encouraged to step outside our comfort zone and keep learning – no matter how wealthy, or not, our parents may be. And truly believing that you are capable of anything comes with a huge level of responsibility to improve your own potential. It is this level of responsibility that is too much for most people. They like to have a permanent excuse that explains where they are in the world. You know: "I didn't go to the right school; I don't know the right people; I wasn't born into a wealthy family; I've had to deal with great tragedy in my life" and so on. Excuses lead to resentment, resentment leads to

ideas generation

bitterness, and bitterness will stop any chance of a creative idea bubbling to the surface... No more excuses!

An idea is like an onion. In the middle there is the core that never changes. We call this The Mother Thought or 'TMT' for short. This part of the idea should be both explosive and nurturing (hence the nickname). But then there are layers and layers of smaller ideas that we call Pilot Thoughts. These little gems exist to illuminate, challenge and protect the TMT. And here's the kicker. Pilots can be changed a million times over without affecting the TMT. We even take pilots from other TMTs and force fit them as experiments.

There is a trick to all of this and you'll be happy to know that there are short cuts. The first trick to learn involves changing the way you think of an idea.

TIP # 1: Never again say you have an idea.

People don't have ideas, they have TMTs! People have half ideas. How many times have you heard the phrase "I have half an idea"? Acknowledging that you have TMTs instead of ideas means that you have acknowledged that ideas are complex things. TMTs are the pure incarnation at the centre of an idea, which is always more complex in the end. You see, an idea has two lives and always lives in two worlds. It has one life in isolation where it exists as an entity and another where it interacts with the real world. Ideas are two things at their very basic level.

Ideas also change and mutate. The biggest mistake people make when thinking about their ideas is that they picture them as complete in theory and all that needs to happen is for the idea to be 'brought to life'. This is not necessarily the case. A good example is the simple packet cake. What a great idea that was! Imagine the first person who thought of the concept of creating a packet cake. Imagine how many people thought that the idea would be a flop. Well in this case both parties were right. The idea of a packet cake wasn't a flop, but the idea in its original shape was a complete flop.

Ideas all follow a similar pattern. Once the value of the concepts or blueprint or formula is established, players in this new economy of ideas actively (and loudly!) claim rights to them.

Not convinced yet?

Well think about it this way.

Public domain know-how has now become a much sought-after prize. Individuals battle for private control of every 'good idea'. Many commentators believe that these knowledge assets will increasingly be snapped up into private hands with hardly a murmur from a largely unsuspecting public – and that this public will remain, for the most part, barely aware of the situation.

In the new economy the really smart players are fast becoming knowledge moguls – technological titleholders who control rights to new processes and products.

Let's look at one case study of a person who truly understood the value of an idea.

Jerome Lemelson was the most prolific individual inventor of modern times. Scores of wealthy people have made masses of money from shipping companies, oil wells, chain stores and buildings, but what he owned was ideas. By the time he died in 1995 at the age of seventy-four, he had registered more than five hundred patents. He was a massive reserve of ingenious ideas. In fact, he was ranked only second to Thomas Edison in the number of US patents he had registered.

ideas generation

Yet most of Lemelson's ideas and inventions are so conceptual that he would be hard pressed to bring any of them to display at the annual Inventors' Expo.

Lemelson presided over a knowledge empire. He built a multimillion-dollar enterprise that produces few products and employs even fewer workers. Whilst other great minds like Alexander Graham Bell and Thomas Edison ran laboratories, Lemelson relied instead on his imagination and his handwritten notebooks of ideas. Like American Express, he never left home without it.

His inventions didn't spawn a vast corporate empire bearing his name, as did those of other inventors. He was always happy to stay in the background. Here's a list of all the things his very big ideas brain thought up.

- Lemelson patented the "recognition tones" that allow fax machines to reliably communicate with each other, earning him royalties from virtually every fax machine manufacturer in the world.
- He staked a claim on a component of the barcode scanning machines that are now at almost every supermarket in the Western world.
- He patented the machine vision used by robots on many of the world's assembly lines.
- He filed for patents on the idea of a video camcorder in the mid-1970s, almost a decade before the product appeared on the market. He even patented the concept of the tape-drive mechanism that engineers ultimately built into the Sony Walkman – a development that won him a lucrative licensing arrangement with Sony and 105 other companies.
- He patented the illuminated highway markers.
- He patented medical procedures for treating brain cancer.

But perhaps his greatest genius was in understanding how to make money on the ownership rights to intangible ideas. Lemelson thought up and laid legal claim to key technological advances that contributed to many of today's high-tech consumer goods. But Lemelson himself rarely translated his ideas into actual products. The embryonic quality of his ideas, rather than from the products themselves, was one of his hallmarks.

It also marks a problem inherent in the knowledge-based economy. Who owns an idea? In Chapter 10, we will take a closer look at ways of protecting ideas and claiming intellectual property rights.

2

Why ideas are like cancer and how to control them

A look at managing the ideas process for both business and personal use.

At Pophouse, we firmly believe that ideas are like cancer. Why? Because ideas will eat you alive unless they are taken out of your head, put down on paper and worked upon. They will grow and fester in your mind and cause destruction unless they are managed, catalogued and, if they're any good, realised.

Unrealised ideas or even those not put on the table for discussion, we believe, will make you sick. An idea that is locked in your memory bank will at first only make you mentally unwell but will slowly begin to undermine your physical health.

Ever heard about the person who had a great idea but never talked about it, worked it through or gave it the opportunity to become a reality? You're probably sitting next to one right now. They become boring. They say things like *"If only, what if, I had that idea first, I knew it could have worked, I could have been famous, I could have been a millionaire, someone else stole my idea."*

We're not suggesting that every idea you have will work or will be brilliant. In fact many, if not most of them, will be terrible. We know that many of ours have been awful! We're saying that you need to give every idea you have the chance to breathe, to be free, to live out in the open. Think of your idea like a teenager. At some point every parent needs to let their child grow up, exist in the real world, survive without intervention. There's no way of knowing whether that child will prosper or whether it needs further guidance and attention. The only way of knowing how strong that child is, is to set it free and see how it survives in the 'real' world.

The only way of knowing whether the child's parents have done a 'quality job' is to put that child's development, principles and values to the ultimate test – freedom.

So you need to set your ideas free. See how they evolve and how they stand up to scrutiny. See if they fall over at the first sight of criticism. See if they have a market. See if they fill a need or create a need. See if they are worthy of further time investment.

The Ideas Process

In the Pophouse method there are five phases of the ideas process. Each phase has some very specific techniques that can be used to manage the ideas process for both personal and business ideas generation.

At the beginning of the 21st century, the line between personal and business becomes even more blurred.

2 Why ideas are like cancer and how to control them

Although you may think you are using this ideas process to generate ideas in your business life, you may have come up with an idea that you can workshop in your personal life.

When Jerome Lemelson came up with the bullseye game using a bullseye board and balls covered in velcro, the idea was inspired from looking at his wife's velcro belt. This is a classic example of how something very personal inspired a great business idea. The velcro game became a worldwide bestseller.

The five phases of the ideas process, in order, are:

1. Prepare
2. Construct
3. Incubate
4. Adjudicate
5. Act

What we mean is:

1. **Prepare**: You find every stimulus material and tool you need to come up with ideas.
2. **Construct**: You build as many ideas as possible.
3. **Incubate**: You allow your ideas to cook and simmer in your subconscious for while.
4. **Adjudicate**: You evaluate your ideas to determine which are the best.
5. **Act**: You take action on your best ideas and turn them into realities.

PHASE ONE: PREPARE

Read, Tear and Study
Before you start coming up with ideas, you should first prepare yourself by reading everything you can get your hands on, tearing out from newspapers or magazines any piece of information that inspires you and that can be pulled out at a later date. You should study like crazy.

Let's say you are going to be trawling for ideas in the fast-food area.

Learn everything you can about the fast-food industry.
Throw yourself into it.
Immerse yourself in all the information you can.
Visit as many fast-food facilities as possible.
Eat as many fast-food meals as you can (it's all research!)
Talk to as many people as possible who work in the fast-food industry and are affiliated with it.

Inspiration usually only strikes those who have immersed themselves in a subject. People are often inspired when they feel confident about the subject matter they are generating ideas about.

It takes input to generate output. In order to feel confident and, more importantly, recognise great ideas, it helps enormously when you first study your subject matter thoroughly.

Ideas favour a fertilised and prepared mind.

Produce – a Lot!
One hundred-metre runners training for the Olympic Games run thousands of hundred-metre races in order to run that one perfect hundred-metre race. These champions race constantly, in order to get to that one great

race – maybe even the one that wins them the Olympic gold medal.

The same is true for ideas. You need to produce a lot of them in order for some of them to be winners. This is one situation where quantity counts and when quantity can actually yield quality.

The more ideas you produce, the more GOOD ideas you're likely to end up with.

When producing ideas, make sure you focus on the quantity, not the quality. We'll worry about the evaluation process later. Your first goal is to give yourself as many alternatives as possible. After all, how can you know if you have a good idea unless you have others to compare it with?

Don't stop after producing what you think might be a promising idea. Instead, acknowledge it and move on. You might actually come up with a better idea in the next five minutes of thought!

The Winner Ideas

Often the ideas you come up with last are most worthy of further investigation.

Why?

Because often the first ideas are lazy ideas, the obvious ideas, the generic ideas. But you need to go through the process of discarding so that you will be able to empty all the very average ideas out of your head, leaving more room for true inspiration. The process will also force you to start searching your brain for the less obvious ideas, those that seem off the wall and a little crazy.

It's OK if these ideas seem wild and impossible to get off the ground. Remember – we're still only generating ideas, not worrying whether they can exist in the real world.

ideas generation

ALWAYS carry a pen!
Never leave home without a pen. You never know when a great idea will strike. Even if it is only a sketchy thought, you need to get it down on paper. Use lipstick if you have to!

If you don't write your idea down immediately, you may lose it forever. Nothing feels worse than a lost idea – it could have been the one that made you a million.

Use a Stepladder to a Better Idea
Sometimes when you're trying to come up with one idea, think about a related subject and see if that unlocks the door to your creativity. Let yourself come up with totally wild and completely impractical ideas.

Let's look at a practical example. Imagine you are a parking attendant. Your parking garage doesn't have enough room for a two-way lane in the middle. It is always a tight squeeze and it is only a matter of time before one of the parked cars is hit. At first you start to think about widening the lanes by removing some of the parking spots – but this will reduce your revenue.

You think, "What if we turned the two entrances and two exits into one-way entrances and exits?" In other words, when drivers enter the carpark, the traffic is one-way. When they exit the carpark, the exit is one way as well. They can only enter from one of the streets and they can only exit from another. Problem solved.

Let your mind seek a new frame of reference. They can stimulate you into thinking up practical ideas.

Create Your Environment to Suit Your Style
Be sure to create your own environment so that you are stimulated, comfortable and conscientious. Do whatever

you need to do to stir up your creativity. Here is a list for you to consider:

- Play music you love (whenever we play 'Walking on Sunshine' by Katrina and the Waves, we can't help but feel a sense of infectious fun and crazy creativity).
- Buy yourself some computer games and a console.
- Surround yourself with soft toys or giant blow up furniture – or any type of toy for that matter. Whatever it takes for you to feel like a child again. It's no secret that children are the most creative beings alive.
- Wear clothes that you like yourself in. Dig out the old pair of tracksuit pants and university sweat shirt.

Find Your Creative Rhythm

What time of day do you tend to get your most creative ideas? Are you a morning thinker or an evening thinker? Make it a priority to discover your most productive time. Take advantage of this creative time by organising your work schedule around it. This will maximise the number of creative ideas you get.

PHASE TWO: CONSTRUCT

Cross-Pollinate Your Ideas
The way to cross-pollinate ideas is to take an idea from one area and apply it to another. Creative ideas come about by combining already existing ideas in a new way.

Learn what others are doing, borrow from them and adapt their ideas to your situation.

The best way to cross-pollinate ideas is to leave your area of specialisation, hunt for ideas in other areas, and then return to your area to apply those ideas.

Be on the lookout for novel connections to your area in other trades, fields, and disciplines. Read broadly and don't limit your exposure to any ideas because you never know where a great one is hiding. The more diverse the places you look for ideas, the more innovative they'll be.

By learning more about different subjects, you'll have more ideas in your mental arsenal with which to make more combinations. Aristotle wrote about philosophy, political theory, theology, economics, botany, sociology, physics and biology. Leonardo Da Vinci was a painter, sculptor, architect, engineer, scientist, musician, theatrical designer, naturalist and inventor.

Do Everything in Reverse
In order to build fresh ideas, try reversing your viewpoint. When you shift your focus to the opposite side of a situation, you steer your thinking in a new direction. And it's in this new direction that you can often come up with creative ideas related to your situation that you would otherwise overlook.

Yin and yang are two principles in Chinese philosophy that represent the opposite forces in the universe: passive and active, negative and positive, feminine and masculine, and so forth. They're based on the concept that the universe is composed of dualistic or two-sided parts that are complementary and contrasting. What one side lacks, the other makes up for. Neither side can exist without its opposite because they're related. Because opposite forces are related, you can often come up with new ideas by looking at the opposite side of your situation.

Before 1968, all high jumpers at the Olympic Games used the same style of jumping. They would spring forward like Superman and clear the bar while facing down towards the ground.

Enter Dick Fosbury. In 1967, Fosbury used the same style of jumping as all the other high jumpers. That year he was ranked forty-eighth in the world. In 1968 he used the technique of reversing to create a new style of jumping which allowed him to go with his natural body instincts. Instead of clearing the bar with his *face down toward the ground*, he turned his body around and cleared the bar with his *face towards the sky*. That year he revolutionised high jumping and won the Olympic gold medal. The best high jumpers of today are still using his technique, which is called the 'Fosbury flop'.

Be Constantly Curious
Ask a lot of questions. Each time you ask a new one, you discover a new answer: New questions steer your thinking in new directions.

There's an art to asking questions. Often, it's more difficult to come up with great questions than great answers. It takes a lot of imagination to create great questions. Since the answer you get depends on the question you ask, a great question will often trigger a great answer.

ideas generation

Instead of seeking only the answers, spend your time more productively by first finding the questions.

Great answers aren't created, they're revealed by great questions.

Pretend

In order to spark fresh ideas, try pretending. When you pretend to be someone else, you gain new insights into your situation. Choose people, living or dead, who you think could achieve your objective. Put yourself in their shoes and try to view your situation from their perspective. Imagine how they would go about achieving your objective. Visualise in your mind's eye what they would do. If you're in the field of physics, pretend you're Albert Einstein. If you're into philosophy, view your situation from Plato's perspective. To develop an idea related to computers, imagine you're Bill Gates.

Instead of choosing famous people, you may want to assume the viewpoint of someone you deal with on a daily basis. If you own a business, try viewing it through your customers' eyes. If you want a view with no inhibitions, look through the eyes of a child.

Imagine the Impossible

Use your imagination to build creative ideas. "What if?" is a great question to ask to spark your imagination.

You might ask yourself questions like, "What if there were twenty-six hours in a day?" or "What if we walked on our hands instead of our feet?" or "What if underwear could also be used as a hat?"

Don't be concerned if your 'what if' questions seem impossible. They can still benefit you by steering your thinking in new directions. Just because something doesn't

2 Why ideas are like cancer and how to control them

currently exist in reality, doesn't mean it couldn't in the future.

Let's examine some 'what if' question asked in the past that seemed impossible at the time:

- What if man could fly in a powered heavier-than-air aircraft? (Orville and Wilbur Wright, engineers)
- What if continents exist beyond Europe? (Christopher Columbus, explorer)
- What if there was a method of inducing immunity to specific diseases? (Edward Jenner, pioneer of vaccination)
- What if sound could be mechanically recorded and reproduced? (Thomas Edison, inventor)
- What if pictures could be transmitted electronically through the air? (Philo T. Farnsworth, pioneer of television)
- What if some sort of device could launch man into space? (Robert Goddard, pioneer of rocketry)

When All Else Fails, Laugh

Laughing is a great way to stimulate creative thinking. You can come up with a lot of fresh ideas while laughing, joking, playing around, goofing off, getting crazy, and not taking yourself too seriously.

Why do you get lots of new ideas when you're fooling around and acting like a kid? The reasons are simple. You're not worried about being useful, being wrong, breaking rules or looking silly. You also drop your inhibitions and loosen up. Creativity thrives in a relaxed mind.

ideas generation

There's a link between humour and creativity. Humour breaks you out of predictable patterns and hits you with the unexpected. It makes your mind flexible and forces you to look at something in an entirely new way. This is, in fact, exactly how fresh ideas come about.

When others see you playing around, they assume you're wasting time or being unproductive. Quite the contrary. Work and play are not opposites. The distinction between them is vague. In fact, if you break down the word recreate, you end up with *re-* which means anew, and *create*, which means to originate. Therefore when you recreate, you originate new ideas.

How to loosen up?

It's good to watch children because they've mastered the art of playing. Children spend most of their time having fun and joking around. They even make games out of any chores they have to do. The great thing about children is that they haven't learned all of the rules yet, so almost anything goes. Because of these qualities, children are a highly creative group.

Be Lean

You can build new ideas by reducing your situation down to its essential components. Often, less is more.

In 1920, Earle Dickinson was working for Johnson & Johnson. At the time, they were producing large surgical bandages for use in hospitals and on battlefields. Dickson's wife was inexperienced and accident-prone in the kitchen. She often burned and cut her hands. The bandages produced by Johnson & Johnson were too big to put on her wounds. So one day Dickson invented smaller bandages for her. Shortly thereafter, Johnson & Johnson began selling a new product called Band-Aids.

Get Expansive

You can build fresh ideas by expanding on the components of your situation. Ask yourself, "How can this be expanded? What can be added?"

When Engineer Gottlieb Daimler asked himself how he could expand the format of the car, he built the first truck.

Rearrange

Break down your situation and list its various components. Then rearrange those components. Put them together in new ways.

What would happen if you moved things around? What if you interchanged the components? What other layout can you create? What other sequence? What's first? Last? In the middle? On top? On the bottom? Where's the beginning? The ending?

Many companies have become wealthy by using reverse engineering. This is the process of taking apart a competitor's product, like a computer, and rearranging its components to create a new product.

Attack From Every Angle

Mentally walk around your situation to get new vantage points or perspectives on it. Shift your frame of reference. You can see your situation differently by surveying it from an unfamiliar angle.

One of the many innovative film techniques developed by Orson Welles in his film *Citizen Kane* was to take camera shots from the ceiling, from beneath the floor, from over the actors' shoulders, and from many other unusual viewpoints.

ideas generation

Check Under Your Nose
Ask yourself whether you're overlooking the obvious idea.

Is it right in front of you? Is it in plain view? Is it right under your nose? Or have you been too busy looking for ideas elsewhere to even notice?

NASA developed the Astronaut Pen in the 1960s so that astronauts could write while is space. It's the only ballpoint pen that can write in zero gravity. All other ballpoint pens need gravity in order for their ink to flow. The Astronaut Pen cost over $1 million to develop. The Soviet Union, however, did not spend $1 million dollars to develop an Astronaut Pen because they saw the obvious solution to writing in zero gravity: They gave pencils to their astronauts.

See the Big Picture
Step back from your situation to see the big picture. When you're too close, you only see the details. Stepping back gives you a fresh perspective.

Inventor Eli Whitney became a pioneer of mass production by manufacturing interchangeable parts which were exactly alike so that unskilled labourers could assemble those parts into products. This process of standardising all parts led to modern assembly-line production. Whitney realised that standardising the parts used in manufacture was not only beneficial to the production process, but it also simplified future maintenance.

Make an Analogy
In order to build fresh ideas, make an analogy for your situation. The best kind of analogy is a metaphor, which

is a figure of speech containing an implied comparison, in which a word or phrase ordinarily and primarily used for one thing is applied to another; for example, 'The law is an ass' or 'Australia rides on the sheep's back'.

Metaphors are effective because they relate new things to what you already know. They make it easier to understand complicated concepts. When you encounter a new concept, it's useful to try to see it in a familiar way by using the known to connect you with the unknown. Familiar concepts help you to comprehend unfamiliar ones through the elements they have in common. For example, the telephone was initially referred to as the 'speaking telegraph'.

Create a metaphor for your situation by finding similarities between seemingly unrelated concepts. How is running a business like juggling? How is communicating like playing tennis? How is teaching a classroom full of children like being a drill sergeant? Metaphors are great mind-joggers because they give you fresh perspectives.

Visual metaphors are the best because they're easy to remember. It's far easier to picture and remember tangible images like a crocodile, a whale, and a duck than vague concepts like aristocracy, phenomenon, and resource. Try to link your situation to a visual metaphor.

Find Other Uses
Change the context of an object or situation so that it takes on a different use, purpose, or meaning. You may not even realise it, but you've been changing the context of things for your entire life. You do this every time you use a newspaper as an umbrella, an inner tube as a raft, or a shoe as a fly swatter.

ideas generation

Shift your focus. Look at the same old thing in new ways. See it in a different light. Ask yourself how it can be put to other uses. What else can you do with it? How can it be reformed? How else can it be classified? What other category can you put it into? What attributes or characteristics of it are you overlooking?

One way to reframe your situation and put it into a different category is to change its name – call it something else, try finding substitutes for the words that describe your situation. Certain meanings and contexts are associated with certain words. So if you shift your focus to alternative words, you'll steer your thinking in different directions. Doing this enables you to change the context of your situation and see it in a different way.

For example, suppose you're an engineer who's trying to improve the aerodynamics of a car. If you substitute the word *vehicle for car*, you'll increase your available options. If you're only thinking car, you'll only analyse the aerodynamics of other cars. However, if you're also thinking vehicle, you'll also analyse the aerodynamics of various vehicles: sleds, spaceships, bicycles, skateboards, rockets and so forth. Analysing these vehicles may lead you to creative ideas that you would have otherwise overlooked.

While hiking in the mountains of Switzerland, engineer George de Mestral became irritated by the burrs that kept clinging to his pants. When he returned home, he examined the burrs under a microscope and discovered that they clung to things because they were covered with hundreds of little hooks. It occurred to him that this burr-clasping system could be put to another use in the form of a new kind of fastener. He called his invention Velcro. Secretary Bette Nesmith looked at a bottle of nail polish and saw a different us for it. Instead of using the bottle to apply nail polish, Nesmith thought about using it to apply a different kind of paint. When she filled it with white tempera paint, she created the first bottle of correction fluid. She called it Liquid Paper.

Try Random Approaches

- Go through a dictionary and pick words at random. Try to apply each word to your situation. Find a connection between them. Ask yourself how each word can enable you to view your situation differently.
- Another way to trigger your imagination is to use visual stimuli. Scan the photographs in magazines and be on the lookout for ways to link them to your situation.
- When you use random words and images, your thinking is steered in a direction it typically would not be. This enables ideas to emerge that otherwise would not.

The key factor is the fact that the selection is *random*. Most people continue to view their situation in the same way, which does not lead them to any new ideas. It takes some form of *random* stimulation to knock them off their current path so they can think differently.

Using seemingly irrelevant words or images to stimulate your thinking does not guarantee that you'll come up with ideas. If you want guaranteed ideas, use relevant words or images. But there's a price to be paid for this guarantee: mediocre ideas. For it's only by exploring the least likely pathway of seemingly irrelevant words or

ideas generation

images that you can expect to come up with the *best possible* ideas.

It's not always easy to find connections between your situation and a random word or image. Occasionally, you'll want to skip one that appears to be unrelated to your situation and go on to a different word or image. Do *not* skip it. Hang in there and force a connection. If you search hard enough, you'll eventually discover a link between the two.

It's usually those words or images that at first seem to be most unrelated and irrelevant to your situation that end up stimulating you into coming up with the best and most creative ideas.

PHASE THREE: INCUBATION

Taking a Mental Recess
Pause take a break, and relax – do not rush in to judging your ideas. Take a mental recess. Do something totally different and unrelated to your objective.

When you relax, creative ideas start to percolate in your head. Breaks allow you to gain a fresh perspective. They also let ideas catch up to you. Your brain needs a chance to process and digest information.

Put your objective on your mental back burner. When you give your mind input in the form of an objective, all you have to do is wait and it'll give you output in the form of ideas.

While your conscious mind relaxes, your subconscious mind works on finding connections between ideas. Your subconscious can piece together any mental puzzle you're working on because it specialises in seeing the big picture. It will work day and night until it pieces together your mental puzzle. So relax and be patient: the ideas will come to you.

If you're in a hurry to achieve your objective, you may feel as if you don't have time to sit on your ideas. The fact of the matter is you don't have time *not* to. The best time to take a break is when you feel that you don't have time for it.

Don't force your way by just ploughing through. You'll be far more effective and efficient if you stop focusing on your objective for a while. When you try forcing your way, you typically end up getting stuck. It's just like getting snowed in. You can either head out into the blizzard and get stuck in the middle of nowhere, or you can wait for the snow to melt and simply drive away. Just because you're active doesn't mean you're accomplishing anything. There's no glory in being a workaholic who does a lot of busy work. You want to be effective and efficient.

Don't feel guilty in taking breaks and relaxing. The time you spend sitting on your ideas is just as important as the time you spend consciously working on them.

The combination of hard work and relaxation delivers the best results and enables you to perform at your optimum level of productivity.

Idea-Friendly Activities

Certain relaxing activities tend to be more stimulating to creative thinking than others. They are:
- **Showering and bathing**
- **Sleeping**
- **Daydreaming**
- **Driving**
- **Exercising**

ideas generation

There's a good reason why these particular relaxing activities tend to stimulate creative thinking the most: They're routine and mindless activities that bore the left side of your brain. When your left side gets bored, it dozes off to a certain degree. This enables your right side, which is your creative side, to kick in and operate freely without being inhibited by your left side.

It was while taking a bath that the Greek mathematician Archimedes discovered the solution to a difficult problem that he had been pondering: how to determine the purity of gold. He discovered how to do this by applying the principle of specific gravity, which states that a body displaces an amount of water equal to its own volume. The moment he made this discovery, he jumped out of his bath and exclaimed, "Eureka!"

While you're sleeping, your subconscious mind continues to work on your objective. It never rests. You can actually reap creative ideas while you sleep. Keep a notepad and a pen next to your bed so you can capture any ideas you get. The best times to capture ideas are immediately before you fall asleep and immediately after you wake up. During these moments you're in a semiconscious state called reverie, which is similar to daydreaming.

When illumination strikes during the creative process, a light goes on inside your head and a bright idea pops up. Illumination is an instant flash of insight that shows a familiar situation in a new light. It's a breakthrough that occurs when the mental puzzle you've been working on suddenly falls into place. In order for illumination to occur, you first have to immerse yourself in your objective. That enables your subconscious mind to wrestle with your objective while you're relaxing and thinking about other things. Then when you least expect it, a bright idea pops up.

PHASE FOUR: ADJUDICATE

You should be selective when it comes to picking out your best creative ideas. After you build lots of ideas and sit on them for awhile, you should judge them and pick out the winners.

Evaluate your ideas to see which are the most practical, feasible, and marketable. Before investing your time, energy and resources into your ideas, you want to weigh their chances for success and assess the risks involved in implementing them.

The goal of the first three phases of the creative process has been to *increase* the number of ideas you have. Conversely, the goal of the 'adjudication' phase is to *decrease* the number. This is achieved by eliminating the losers and keeping the winner. During this phase, you should stop focusing on quantity and start focusing on quality.

Analysis and Intuition

There are two methods of judging ideas: by analysis and by intuition. Analysis relies on your brain. Intuition relies on your instinct.

There are numerous ways of analysing ideas. One is to perform a small-scale test. Organisations often test-market new products and services in a small market before expanding to a national market.

Another is to list their advantages and disadvantages. Then choose the idea that has the highest number of advantages in proportion to disadvantages.

Sometimes too many factors are involved to be able to judge the practicality of your ideas with any accuracy. That's when you need to follow your intuition. Did you

ideas generation

ever get a hunch that something just feels right, even though there's little evidence to support it? Did you ever arrive at a decision without knowing any of the steps that you took to get there? Did you ever get a sense of knowing something without any logical reason for knowing? That's intuition.

Intuition lets you know when you're on the right track. How does it work? Your subconscious mind records every bit of data you encounter. Then it makes connections among these bits of data and forms the basis for hunches. Intuitive leaps bypass the logical steps it usually takes to reach a decision. In other words, your intuition takes shortcuts.

How did Thomas Edison judge the worthiness of his ideas? He developed his guidelines for judging ideas immediately after his first patent, for a vote recorder, didn't sell. From then on he vowed never again to work on an invention that the public didn't want and he couldn't sell. He decided to first find out what would sell and then to go about inventing it.

After inventor Alfred Nobel created dynamite and other explosives, he felt embittered because they were used as weapons. So to make himself feel better, he used the profits from his inventions to create the charitable Nobel Foundation. Nobel did an excellent job of judging his ideas on the basis of how much money they would bring him. Unfortunately, he did not do as well at judging how he would feel about the results.

Listen to an Outsider
Explain your objective and ideas to an outsider: Find someone with a fresh eye who's unfamiliar with your situation. Ask for his or her viewpoint. Seek constructive criticism.

An outsider may point out something that you've been completely overlooking.

Your perspective is limited when you're inside the situation looking out. Someone who's outside the situation can help you establish a new frame of reference.

Seek the point of view of a child. It's not unusual for children to see ideas in totally different ways. Children often spot things that adults don't because they aren't aware of the traditional ways of viewing a particular situation.

Besides a child, ask someone from a different trade, field or discipline. Ask someone who's not an expert in your area and is far removed from your situation for views on your ideas. Use his or her inexperience to your advantage. Unlike an expert, a novice does not have preconceived notions; he or she has not become educated about what is and what is not possible and will therefore consider more options than an expert.

Just because you listen to an outsider's opinion of your ideas doesn't mean that you have to follow the advice. The purpose of listening to an outsider is to gain a fresh perspective on the quality of your ideas.

PHASE FIVE: ACT

Put it All on the Line

After you've judged your ideas, take action on the winners.

There comes a time when you have to go for it. No guts, no glory. Don't become a victim of paralysis by analysis. To have great ideas and not to take action on them is exactly the same as not having any ideas at all. They both yield the same results – none.

ideas generation

Do Not Make Excuses For Not Taking Action

Some people who are creative at coming up with ideas are even more creative at making up excuses for not acting on them. One of their most common excuses is that their idea is not yet perfect. So they procrastinate.

Procrastinators choose to wait until everything is perfect. But there will never be a right time. You'll never have all of the answers. There will *always* be some kind of obstacle in the way. Once you take action, you can always correct any flaws in your ideas. Many times you won't even realise that flaws exist until your ideas are put into action. Work for progress, not perfection.

Begin!

Another excuse people often create for not acting on their ideas is that they don't believe that they're capable of coming up with *great* ideas. Have you ever rejected your own thoughts before somebody else had a chance to? As soon as you get a new idea, your subconscious mind will create all kinds of reasons why it is bound to fail. Your subconscious will tell you that you can't do it or that you're not smart enough.

Life is all About Attitude

Imagine for a moment that you're lying on your deathbed. As you reflect on your life, you regretfully think: "I could have...," "I should have...," "If only I had..." You realise that you've gone throughout life holding back. You haven't given it your best shot or followed through on some of the things you really wanted.

Nobody else has your great ideas. Nobody else can bring them to life, nobody but you. Act on them so that we can all benefit.

3
Breaking the rules

How to overcome the obstacles the world puts in your way

As human beings, it is in our nature to oppose change. Not only do we oppose it, we do everything in our power to avoid it. Do not be shocked and hurt that the world puts obstacles in your way – deliberately!

The world is full of people who will oppose your idea, are uncomfortable with the notion of your success and don't want to face something new. Learning doesn't appear to be our greatest strength.

There are countless rules and social norms we are expected to obey. Some are to promote a civilised society, others exist simply to keep us all in our places.

Learning how to successfully break the rules will help to climb to new heights in generating ideas. Here are some of the most important rules you will need to remember as you create your unique ideas.

ideas generation

Break Away From Internal Criticism
You must break away from your internal critic. It's the negative part of you that prejudges and rejects new ideas before they get off the ground.

When you're building creative ideas, don't judge them right away. Criticism plays a vital role in the creative process, but there's a time and a place for it. That time and place is during the adjudication phase of the creative process, which begins after you've built lots of ideas.

New ideas rarely arrive as finished products; they have to be moulded, developed and refined. Sometimes when ideas first occur they're only fragments, which can become completed entities only when combined with other idea fragments. Thus, your first impression of new ideas usually is not an accurate one.

You cannot always accurately determine the quality of your ideas when you're in the early phases of the creative process. Often ideas that are seemingly impractical when viewed in the current frame of reference become practical when the frame of reference itself changes. Suspended judgment prevents you from prematurely choking off seemingly impractical ideas.

Ideas that are not useful in themselves may serve as stepping stones that lead to useful ideas.

Break Away From Critical People
When you're building creative ideas, avoid critical people because they're amateurs at creating ideas and professionals at *killing* them.

If you tell critical people your creative ideas and they snicker, roll their eyes, and give you condescending looks, you'll probably get discouraged. Don't allow anybody to squelch your creative ideas. A new idea is delicate. It can be killed very quickly.

Criticism from adults is the main reason that children lose a lot of their creative abilities.

Children start off being highly creative. But the more they get negative feedback from adults, the more they conform.

Leave All Your Options Open
During the creative process, you should consider any choices you happen to find. This is not an indecisive or disorganised thing to do!

Keep an eye focused on what you're trying to accomplish. At the same time, keep another eye on the lookout for possibilities that may pop up unexpectedly during the process.

Many of the great inventions and discoveries came about because someone who was focusing on one thing accidentally stumbled upon something else. These serendipitous inventors and discoverers maintained an open frame of mind and weren't afraid to be led astray from what they were initially trying to do. As a result, they were able to recognise the significance of their unexpected findings and create new inventions or make new discoveries.

It's OK To Do Things Differently
Most people don't like to do things differently. We're creatures of habit who tend to fall into a rut and stay there. Unconsciously, we're accustomed to doing things in fixed and routine ways. Our habits are automatic and almost instinctive. We can become, well, predictable. It's difficult to break the pattern.

ideas generation

Sometimes it's necessary to jog your mind so that you can break free of deeply ingrained habits. Avoid becoming a prisoner of habitual thinking by looking for alternative approaches. The more you get stuck in doing things the same way, the less likely you are to think in a different way. When you do things differently, you interrupt your existing thought patterns so that you can think differently. This enables you to get new ideas.

Getting Out of a Rut and Breaking Rules

To build fresh ideas, you need to climb out of any rut you may be stuck in. You've got to stop digging in the same old hole because that's how you got into the rut in the first place. Your brain needs new stimuli. Make it a point to shake up your routine occasionally, get off the beaten path, change your environment, poke around in new areas, knock yourself out of routine patterns, get a change of scenery and explore unknown places.

You might try to do the following:

- Read about a subject that's totally unfamiliar to you.
- Drive a new way to work to explore the scenic route instead of the speedy one.
- Strike up a conversation with someone you would usually ignore.
- Walk through a shop you normally wouldn't go into.

When it comes to creative thinking, rules can sometimes get in your way because you have to work around them. When you break the rules, you expand your possibilities and come up with more ideas. You become free to look for answers 'outside the box'. Don't be afraid to break the rules every once in a while.

Sometimes it no longer makes sense to follow a rule. This occurs when its original purpose for existing has long since vanished. As time passes, and the reason for the creation of the rule becomes obsolete, we continue to follow it because it's still a rule. When asked why we're doing something a certain way, we often mindlessly respond, "Because that's the way we've always done it."

Breaking the rules is one of the ways that you can create. Progress in every trade, field, and discipline occurred when some great independent thinker questioned the status quo and broke the rules. Instead of doing things the same old way, these thinkers made breakthroughs by trying a different approach.

To create something new, one must first destroy what existed before it. Once freed from obsolete ideas, new ones can be created to replace them.

- Walt Disney broke the rule that animated cartoons must be silent.
- Fred Smith broke the rule that only the US Post Office can deliver mail in the US when he founded Federal Express.
- Computer entrepreneur Steve Jobs, inventor George Eastman and inventor Isaac Singer broke the rule that computers, cameras, and sewing machines can't be designed for home use and mass-marketed to the consumer.

Challenge Your Assumptions
Just like rules, assumptions inhibit the creative process. Deeply ingrained assumptions actually become invisible boundaries that imprison your thinking. Breaking out of and expanding beyond these self-imposed boundaries will open up many more options for you. Make it a point to challenge your assumptions every now and then. Don't allow them to become immune to scrutiny.

One technique for challenging your assumptions is to repeat the question, "Why?" several times in a row. First state an assumption that you're making. Then ask "Why?" again. And again. This technique prevents you from being satisfied with the standard explanation and enables you to look at your assumptions in a different way.

Develop A Thick Skin
Develop thick skin to protect yourself from the harsh elements of the outside world like critics, cynics, and pessimists. They'll try to prevent your ideas from coming to fruition.

Critics are afraid of new ideas. They're comfortable with the status quo. New ideas put them on the defensive because they perceive them as threats. The more successful you and your ideas become, the more inadequate critics feel in comparison. They become envious because they didn't think of the ideas themselves.

We're referring to the destructive critics here, not the constructive ones. Constructive criticism is a good thing. It plays a vital role when judging ideas. Without it, a lot of time would be wasted by people taking action on average ideas. But destructive criticism serves no useful function.

Negative phrases that critics frequently use are:
"Don't be ridiculous."
"Yes, but...."
"It'll never work."
"We've already tried that."
"You can't do that."
"It won't fly."
"Give it up."
"No."

Here are some inaccurate predictions made by critics:

"There is a world market for maybe five computers." (CEO of IBM, 1942)

"Heavier than air flying machines are impossible." (Lord Kelving, president of the British Royal Society, c. 1895)

"Who the hell wants to hear actors talk!" (Harry Warner, president of Warner Brothers, 1927)

While attending Yale, Fred Smith wrote a paper for his economics class that described his plan to create Federal Express. His professor told him that the idea would never work and gave him a C on the paper.

Be Tough and Fearless

In order to bring your great ideas to fruition, you've got to be persistent!

If your ideas don't fly the first time you act on them, you must have the tenacity to go back to the drawing board, improve on those ideas, and act on them again. And again. And again. Go after your great ideas wholeheartedly with everything you've got. You've got to become an unstoppable force!

Most people fail in life because they quit too easily. When they run up against a temporary defeat, they immediately throw in the towel. What's ironic is that

ideas generation

they're often just inches away from victory and don't realise it when they decide to give up. If they had just hung in there a little bit longer, they could have succeeded.

The first book written by Dr. Seuss was rejected by twenty-seven publishers. Before getting *Chicken Soup for the Soul* accepted, co-authors Jack Canfield and Mark Victor Hansen were rejected by thirty-three publishers.

Country music star Randy Travis spent over ten years at the same nightclub waiting to be discovered. He fried catfish and washed dishes at the nightclub during the day. At night, he sang on stage. His persistence eventually paid off.

Walt Disney, Henry Heinz, and Clarence (Bob) Birdseye didn't give up on success even after going bankrupt.

One young man who desperately wanted to be a writer seemed to have all of the cards stacked against him. He made $60 a week as a laundry worker and lived in a trailer with his wife and child. In order to help put food on the table, his wife worked nights. The laundry worker typed every night and every weekend. He sent his manuscripts to publishers and agents only to be rejected time and time again. In disgust, the laundry worker gave up one night. He threw the manuscript he was working on into the trash. His wife, however, did not allow him to quit. She retrieved his manuscript and told him to finish what he had started. And it's a good thing that she did or Stephen King would never have written *Carrie*, which went on to sell five million copies.

Why Failure is Good

Creativity is risky business. When you do things that have never been done before, it's to be expected that you'll occasionally fail.

3 Breaking the rules

Failure is an important part of the creative process because you learn so much from it.

Once you bring your ideas out here into the real world, they either succeed or they fail. If they succeed the first time out, you're lucky - really lucky. Most ideas are not born as finished products; they have to be moulded, developed, and refined.

Ideas start out as vision. Once acted upon, they are put to the reality test. When ideas go from vision to reality, flaws are often uncovered. You should view these flaws as feedback, not failure. Failure only occurs if you give up on your ideas because they have a few flaws.

Feedback, on the other hand, provides you with the opportunity to respond to any flaws in your ideas by making changes that improve them. Sure, it's painful to get negative feedback. But if you use it to refine your ideas, you can turn that short-term pain into a long-term gain. Sometimes it's necessary to take one step backwards in order to take two steps forward.

Flaws are actually opportunities in disguise. Don't allow negative feedback to make you bitter, allow it to make you better. Learn from your mistakes.

When you do nothing, you learn nothing. But when you try and fail, you learn what doesn't work. That puts you one step closer to what will work. Negative feedback provides you with the opportunity to change your direction, alter your course, and try a different approach. Failure is the best teacher of all. After all, you learn by trial and error.

For the first four years of its existence, the comic strip *Dilbert* ran in fewer than 150 newspapers. It was a failure in the world of syndicated comics. Its creator Scott Adams decided to make a change. He put his e-mail address on *Dilbert*, which enabled his readers to provide him with feedback. Adams immediately discovered that his readers' favourite *Dilbert* strips were the ones about business and technology. He responded by drawing more cartoons about them. As a result, *Dilbert* now runs in over 1700 newspapers and Adams is a multimillionaire.

David McConnell sold books door-to-door. Housewives were not interested in the books and frequently slammed the door in McConnell's face before he had a chance to make his sales pitch. Instead of quitting, McConnell decided to start giving away a free gift so that he would be allowed to make his sales pitch. He chose to give away a small vial of perfume, which he made up himself. He soon discovered that the women preferred the perfume to the books. McConnell stopped selling books and created his own company: Avon.

The best kind of failure is fast failure because it minimises the amount of time, energy and resources you spend on bringing your ideas to life. The faster you can go through the following sequence of events, the more successful you'll be:

1. Take action on your ideas.
2. Receive feedback on your ideas.
3. Respond to the feedback by making changes that improve your ideas.
4. Take action on your improved ideas.

4

Thinking the unthinkable

Tips for keeping your brain in tip-top condition and keeping it thinking originally.

Just to remind you – the brain is the master control centre of the body. It receives, processes, and stores the information that floods into it from inside and outside the body. It is the supreme ruler as it issues thousands of "instructions" for body action and response. It is the seat of human consciousness, intellect, memory, emotions, and personality.

Think of the brain like both a computer and a chemical factory. Your brain cells produce electrical signals and send them from cell to cell along pathways called circuits. As in a computer, these electrical circuits receive, process, store, and retrieve information. Unlike a computer, however, the brain creates its electrical signals by chemical means. The proper functioning of the brain depends on many complicated chemical substances produced by

ideas generation

brain cells. It is without doubt the most sophisticated software and hardware package in the world! We will show you how to keep it in tip-top condition.

Looking after the brain

The brain is always working, even when you're sleeping. It's always yearning for learning, since it's in charge of learning and mastering new things. It's even in control of all your feelings and emotions. Treat your brain well by eating good foods, exercising, and getting enough sleep. Protect your brain by always wearing a helmet when playing sports or riding your bicycle. And don't drink alcohol, take drugs, or use tobacco – the cells in your brain hate this stuff because it kills them. Take care of the boss of your body and it won't let you down – it's the hardest worker around.

Diet and Nutrition

Your brain is a glutton for nourishment. Although it represents only about 2 per cent of you body weight, it uses more than 20 per cent of your energy – consuming half the blood sugar circulating in your bloodstream, one-quarter of your nutrients, and one-fifth of all the oxygen you inhale.

Your brain is dense. Its immense complexity and density are only made possible by the intricate network of blood vessels and capillaries that deliver the nutrients your brain needs. Optimal blood flow throughout the brain is absolutely essential for its proper function. When the brain's blood vessels are narrowed by disease or its capillaries weakened by poor nutrition, it becomes difficult to effectively and fully nourish the brain. Therefore, the brain is prone to malnourishment even when nutritional levels are adequate for the rest of the body.

Your brain has a sweet tooth. Glucose is the main fuel brain cells use. Unfortunately, brain cells cannot store glucose. They depend on the bloodstream for a constant supply of glucose and oxygen. Two fixtures in our society, stress and sugar, each cause reactions that lower the amount of glucose available to the brain. In excess, they also damage the brain, especially its ability to remember and learn.

The trouble is that even in the best of times your brain is often malnourished, which is then reflected in your mood and emotions, and by your thoughts and behaviour. Fortunately, your brain quickly responds to proper nutrition – even from a single meal – so what are you going to feed your brain today?

The Brain Food Pyramid

A fit and healthy brain depends on a combination of nutrients that support the structural integrity, electrical activity, and growth of cells. Nutrients enable it to synthesise the chemical messengers it uses for intercellular communication. Nutrients power and protect it.

Because a malnourished brain alters mood and behaviour, the best possible nourishment has the potential to get at the root of social problems stemming from fear, apathy, anger and violence. As research unveils the complex biochemistry of the human brain and the intimate connection between what we eat and what we create, this knowledge can enable us to function at our best. We can then explore our full cognitive potential for a richer life – positively influencing individual evolution and planetary health.

ideas generation

Brain nutrition has four primary aspects, each corresponding to a class of food. Like the sides of a pyramid, they work together to create, protect, power, and activate your brain.

- **Structure:** fats for essential fatty acids and cell membrane integrity
- **Protection:** fruits and vegetables for antioxidants and brain cell longevity
- **Energy:** Carbohydrates for glucose and energy production
- **Function:** Proteins for amino acids and neuro transmitter synthesis

Basically, you need essential fatty acids to build your brain, antioxidants to safeguard it, glucose to fuel it, and amino acids to interconnect it.

Exercise

The brain hungers for novelty – and exercise!

The human brain is constantly seeking new information. Like a sponge, it desperately wants to finds out new things all the time. This is what turns the brain on.

In response to novelty, the synaptic connections (or 'wires') in the brain are strengthened and different areas of the brain are linked together, producing new patterns of thought and new patterns of connection. All of this can lead to better brain health. But if it was simply more activity in the brain that leads to the production of new brain patterns, then listening to more music would lead to better brain health. Such passive stimulation of the senses, however, doesn't work as a brain exercise and neither does repeatedly doing the same routine activities. So what does?

There are a number of brain exercises or what we like to call 'neurobics' that can keep your brain in tip-top condition. Neurobics is neither passive nor routine. It is an active way of using the five senses in novel ways to break out of everyday routines.

Exercising the five – mostly underused – senses

Our five senses are the portals through which our brain gets its entire contact with the outside world. We rely primarily on our senses of vision and hearing because they quickly tell us a lot about our environment. Our other senses – smell, taste and touch – are less frequently called upon.

To understand this concept better, close your eyes and walk around a room. Instantly the world around you changes radically. With vision gone, your sense of touch suddenly becomes paramount.

The brain has a huge network of pathways based on visual information. That's why the bulk of information in our society is visual and geared toward visual appeal. Think about the hundreds of advertising billboards and television commercials you are exposed to everyday. They are all designed to play on your sense of sight.

The sense of smell is less relevant in our society. Despite its diminished role in daily life however, the sense of smell plays an important role in memory. That's why certain aromas can remind us all of things that happened years ago – childhood, grandmothers, places we used to visit.

The other senses are also underused – touch, taste and feel.

We will give you a whole bunch of exercises to stimulate and 'wake-up' each of these five senses.

Neurobics

Neurobics or neurological aerobics is all about keeping the brain in peak physical condition. There's no need to find extra time to do these exercises or so anything particularly difficult or special. All you need to do is do two things:

- **Experience the unexpected in the course of the day.**
- **Use all five senses in the course of the day.**

The truth about exercise is that you need to be extremely motivated to do it and you need to put aside regular time to do it. That's why all of the neurobics exercises we're about to give you are designed to fit into what you do on an ordinary day – waking up, travelling to work, working, eating, shopping or even relaxing.

Just as weight-loss experts advise that losing weight is all about a total and permanent lifestyle shift rather than a crash diet in a minimum length of time, neurobics should be treated as a lifestyle choice. Simply by making small changes in your daily habits, you can turn everyday activities into 'brain-building' exercises.

The entire point of neurobics is to keep your brain alive, to keep it stronger and in better shape as you grow older. Many neurobic exercises challenge the brain by reducing its reliance on sight and hearing and encouraging the less frequently used senses of smell, touch and taste to play a more prominent role in everyday activities. By doing so, rarely activated pathways in your brain's associative network are stimulated, increasing your range of mental flexibility.

So what are the conditions that make an exercise neurobic? It should do one or more of the following:

- **Involve one or more of your senses in a novel context.**
  Blunt the senses you normally use and force your self to rely on your other senses. For example, eat your breakfast with your eyes closed.
- **Engage your attention.**
  Make everyday events and things in your life stand out from the ordinary. For example, turn the picture in your office upside down.
- **Break your daily routine in an unexpected and imaginative way.**
  For example, drive to work taking a completely new route or jump on an inexpensive mystery flight on a weekend.

Like the body, the brain needs a balance of activities. Luckily, ordinary routines present hundreds of opportunities to activate your senses in extraordinary ways. We recommend you don't try using neurobic exercises all day, everyday. Instead, pick one or two things from the menu of exercises – and begin to invent your own exercises.

Morning and evening rituals
Our routines are usually the most ingrained and ritualised in the mornings and evenings. Because this is the case, they are ideal times to inject a touch of novelty to awaken our brain circuits.

- Instead of waking up to the smell of coffee brewing, why not wake up to the smell of peppermint or eucalyptus oil? Place an oil-burner next to your bed. This is a great way to break associative habits of smell.

ideas generation

- Once you've chosen your wardrobe, dress with your eyes closed. This is a great way of relying on your sense of balance and memory of how your shirt is buttoned or tied. (Don't do this if you are in a hurry!)
- Brush your teeth with your non-dominant hand. This exercise requires you to use the opposite side of your brain instead of the one you normally use. Research suggests that doing this on a regular basis can result in a significant expansion of circuits in the brain that control and process tactile information from the hands.
- When you wake, play music in your bedroom that includes sounds of the ocean or a rainforest, rather than waking to the sound of morning radio. This will catch your brain off-guard, as the brain has become used to hearing the same thing every morning.
- Change the order of your morning by doing things like getting dressed before breakfast or eating breakfast before getting dressed. Alternatively, play with your children first thing in the morning before doing anything.
- If you read a book before going to bed, read it aloud to yourself or your partner. When we read aloud, we use quite different brain circuits than when we read silently. Research proves that three distinct regions light up when the same words are spoken, heard or read.

Commuting
It's funny how we all tend to use the same travel route everyday to get to school or work. Rarely do we alter the

route we use, thinking that perhaps it the best or safest or shortest way to get to our intended destination. Normally, it's predictable and boring. If we own a car, we rarely think to take the bus or walk (if we live close enough). We rarely choose to carpool and we almost never drive half of the way, park and take the bus the rest of the way. To some people, that's almost too weird.

Most of the time, the ride to work is spent encased in a coma-like state, shielded from the sights and sounds and smells of the world around us. How often have you heard someone comment on the flowers or express joy in the *actual journey* to work or school?

Yet this is one of the best places to get an amazing neurobic workout and turn the often-mindless activity of travel into a stimulating and intriguing journey. This is a great way to strengthen your brain and get it into tip-top shape.

Here are some ways to start your brain exercise.

- If you drive your car to work, drive in complete silence. When the brain knows the route, it switches to automatic pilot and gets little stimulation.
Take a new route to work and try to stay aware of what you are doing – rather than driving mindlessly. This unfamiliar route will activate the cortex and hippocampus, allowing the brain to process new sights and smells and start to create a new brain map. Notice the new path along the way. Be in the moment.
- If you drive to work maybe you can swap cars with a friend who has a very different car to yours. When you do this, driving will feel different, and your brain can no longer use familiar assumptions for controlling the car.

ideas generation

- If you drive to work, wind the window down and listen to the sounds of the street and smell the seasons in the air. The hippocampus is especially involved in associating odours, sounds and sights to construct mental maps. Opening the windows of your car provides these circuits with more raw materials.
- If you always drive to work, take the bus. Enjoy the experience of letting somebody else drive you to work. Listen to the conversations around you and watch the trees and the scenery go by.
- Why not walk to work? If you live too far away to walk the entire distance, maybe you can walk some of the way. There's something about walking that awakens the senses – all the senses.
- Don't ignore opportunities to be social when commuting. Say hello to the bus driver, say good morning to the person you are sitting next to on the train. Numerous scientific research studies have proven that social deprivation has severe negative effects on overall cognitive abilities. Of course, be sensible and stay away from dangerous-looking people!
- As well as being environmentally sound, car-pooling provides opportunities for some great interaction and lively discussion. It can awaken your mind before you even reach your destination.
- If you choose to catch the train or bus, why not take a sketchpad (or ideas pad) and get inspired by your surroundings?
There is a whole world outside your window ready for you to explore.

At work

Nearly all of us spend roughly half the waking day at work. Work is also the place that we need to be at our best and brightest. We want to appear intelligent and creative at work – particularly in this era of intense competition. We call on our brainpower all day and we want to constantly make the best possible impression.

We don't suggest that you spend your busy day doing numerous exercises to further strain your brain. But we do suggest that you use neurobic exercises to give your brain a break from the mental jobs you are responsible for in your workplace.

- **Change the layout of your office/workstation:** Routine in your workspace has resulted in your cortex and hippocampus constructing a spatial map of everything in your space. Very little mental effort is required to locate objects on your desk so your brain immediately falls into a type of sleepwalking trance. This is the last thing we want! By moving your workspace around you can reactivate special learning networks and get your visual and somatosensory brain areas back to work.
- **Change your daily timetable:** Can you change your lunch hour? Instead of drinking coffee throughout the day, maybe you can change to herbal tea. Can you create a little disorder in your day? Any changes you can incorporate will also reactivate your visual and sensory brain areas and wake them up.
- **Add some colour to your workspace:** Add some pictures or posters or even large pieces of paper

ideas generation

painted in solid, primary colours to your office wall. Colour can evoke very strong emotional associations and create very different feelings about your workday. If you are in a rut, staring into a strong yellow colour is said to stimulate the brain and wake it up.

- **Add some scents to your workspace:** In Japan, nutmeg or cinnamon odours are added to air-conditioning systems of office buildings to enhance productivity. In your own office you can experiment with different scents to activate your memory and help stimulate your creative juices.
- **Use the lift:** Sometimes one of the best ways to gain neurobic exercise is to get in the lift. As much as this next exercise may seem childish, it can work very effectively. Take the lift up to the top floor of your building and press every floor button. The lift will stop at every floor and as the doors open, you will be given a very different perspective. Your senses will be exposed to new sights, sounds and smells. Your neural networks will be exposed to new experiences, even if the differences are subtle.
- **Take a friend or family member to work:** When you have friends or family visiting you in your workplace, it usually means that you have to introduce them to your co-workers. These all-important social interactions are crucial for a healthy brain.
- **Turn your world upside down:** Take something in your office – a picture or an illustration – and turn it upside down. Your brain is quite literally of

4 Thinking the unthinkable

two minds when it comes to processing visual information. The analytical part of your brain – your left brain – will try to label an object after just a brief glance. The right brain in contrast, perceives spatial relationships and uses non-verbal cues. So, for example, when you look at a familiar picture right side up, your left brain quickly labels it and diverts your attention to other things. When the picture is upside down, this strategy doesn't work and your right-brain net work kicks in and takes over the interpretation process. This is a great way to get the neurones in the brain working in a new way.

- **Collect objects and gadgets that stimulate the mind:** Bring in things that seem out of place in the office. Sometimes some of the most stimulating objects are things that children like to play with – soft toys, computer games, building blocks. Keep some playthings in your office at all times. Don't be afraid to play with them. As your brain is not used to 'playing with toys' it will force stimulation in parts of the brain that probably got a lot of use when you were child. 'Regressing' can often be a very healthy exercise for the brain.

Shopping

In the agrarian economy, gathering food gave one an extremely vigorous neurobic workout. Every sense was utilised in hunting animals, planting crops, anticipating the weather and planning for seasonal changes. There was no guarantee of survival and hunger always loomed just around the corner.

ideas generation

As safe and convenient as the supermarket is, it is also predictable and for many, extremely boring. Instead of our five senses being awakened by the smells and sounds and sights of the 'market place', everything is now packaged to within an inch of its life. Food is snap-frozen, canned and pummelled into shape. Even the transaction of food is sterile – no more bartering, just scanning at the supermarket checkout.

Here are some neurobic exercises to do while shopping.

- **Go to a farmers' or fresh produce market.** There's something quite exhilarating about going to a farmers market and experiencing the sights and sounds of 'real food.' You don't even need to go for a reason or with the intention to buy. Browsing is the best way to experience these types of markets. Many of today's farmers markets display the produce in such a way that awakens the senses and the appetite. The food seems to taste different. Taste a cheese that isn't covered in shrink-wrapped packaging, taste a piece of fruit that is in season and has just been picked from a tree. Smell the dirt that still remains in a punnet of strawberries. Buy a tomato vine and grow some fresh fruits or vegetables at home. You might want to choose a type of food you enjoy eating – let's say cheese. Go to the cheese section of the farmers' market and taste all the different types of cheeses. Savour each flavour and allow your tastebuds to distinguish between the different types of cheeses. Ask the stallholder how the cheese is aged. Find out how many years the stall

holder has been in the industry. Ask any questions that come to mind. This exercise is an excellent way to awaken all of the five senses and interact with people you wouldn't normally interact with. It is probably one of our favourites.
- **Shop in another suburb.** One of the best ways to engage in neurobic exercise is to shop in an area you are unfamiliar with. If you haven't before, you may want to try a place like your local Chinatown and shop in a place that offers completely different fruits, vegetables and meats. An Asian or Indian market will offer a wide variety of completely novel foods, visual and olfactory sensations. The olfactory system can distinguish millions of aromas by activating unique combinations of receptors in the nose. Encountering these new aromas adds new chords into the symphony of brain activity. And because this system is linked directly to the emotional centre of the brain, new aromas may evoke unexpected feelings and associations.
- **Shop locally.** Choose the local corner store over the big supermarket. Seek out the neighbourhood butcher, baker and candlestick maker! Ask for recommendations from staff and take in the small businessperson's way of arranging the shop window. Speak to the other customers and get to know the local proprietor.
- **Grow your own food.** We've all thought about growing that little vegetable patch in the backyard. Now's the time to do it! Make friends with your local nursery and seek advice on what to plant and how to plant it. There's nothing quite

like watching Mother Nature close up. The experience of digging up the garden and planting something will awaken the neurones in your brain in ways that *buying* those tomatoes just can't achieve.

Eating

In times gone by we usually sat down to share our daily meals – particularly dinnertime. In the age of busy schedules and fast-food, this rarely happens. Breaking bread and enjoying food is an ideal place to practice neurobic exercises. Every meal provides the opportunity to engage with family and friends. These social interactions have proven positive effects on brain health. Changing how you eat, rather than what you eat, can be highly beneficial for the brain.

- **Take away all the distractions**. Turn off the TV, put away the newspapers, and concentrate on what you are eating. Have your family or friends around the table and enjoy both the conversation and the food. Food can often taste better when it is shared with people for whom you care.
- **Change the scenery.** Take your family and friends on a picnic. Go to your favourite park and enjoy the sounds of your environment along with the company. Listen to the sounds around you. Awaken all five of your senses and give each of them a good neurobic workout.
- **Change where you sit.** At dinnertime, have all of your friends or family switch seats. In most families, everyone has his or her own seat and it

is amazing how permanent these positions can become. Often your position in the family determines the position you are allocated at the table – head of the family usually gets the seat at the head of the table and so on. What would happen if you put the youngest at the head of the table? This arrangement challenges pre-existing notions of seniority and power and ultimately challenges the brain's set patterns of predictability and order.

- **Change the order in which you eat food.**
Try having cereal for dinner or start by having your dessert first and finish with your entrée or appetiser. Challenge your brain's pre-programmed definition of breakfast or when a dessert is eaten.
- **Eat your entire meal with your eyes closed.**
Let the food hit your tastebuds without your eyes identifying what you are eating. Awaken your sense of taste and 'rewire' your brain's pathways when it comes to the order – make taste first, not sight.

Leisure time

Use neurobics in your spare time to make that time more enjoyable. Rather than just flopping down in front of the television set, strike a balance between brain-stimulating neurobic activity and mind-in-idle time.

- **Travel.** No one can overestimate the importance of travel in life. There is so much to see in the world – and so little time to see it! Take as many trips as you can – even the three-day kind where you can experience local places and people. At every point, travel involves something unexpected

ideas generation

for the senses. All those carefully constructed spatial maps no longer apply. Your brain will constantly be moving at top speed – attempting to process local customs and languages.

- **Get involved.** Participate in a community project that has interested you for some time. See things from a community perspective rather than from your own. You will be able to interact with people in your community of a different age or background. Challenge your thinking and pre-conceptions. 'Neurobercise' your brain to see things from a different point of view.
- **Learn something new.** Try taking a course at a community college – something that absolutely terrifies you, such as accounting 101 or calligraphy. Challenge your sense of where you think your talents lie. Open your brain up to new pathways that, for whatever reason, you seem to have locked off forever. Be brave!
- **Drive into the sunset.** Go for a long drive with no particular destination in mind. See where the open road leads you. Maybe drive in a part of your town or city you have always wanted to see. Most of the time when you are in the car you have specific destinations in mind and usually a very predictable way of getting there. When you are not sure of what will come up next in your journey, your brain is far more alert as it begins to process new information. Your attention circuits will be turned up to full volume whilst also exercising your spatial navigation skills. A long, rambling walk will have a similar effect.

There are literally millions of ways of keeping your brain in great shape. The name of the game is continuous learning and exploration. Neurobic exercises should never be thought of as work. They are simply a way for you to get the maximum output from your mind – and let's face it, if you plan on being an ideas generator your whole life, staying in shape is a great idea.

Generating ideas is like running a mental marathon. Keeping your brain in the best shape possible will help you win the race of endurance!

Creativity and the Brain

Almost everyone understands what we mean by creativity. It is something that we are all familiar with – solving a problem, having an idea for a new way to do something, feeling that sudden flash of inspiration when everything falls into place – yet, despite the fact that we have all experienced it at one time or another, creativity remains an elusive phenomenon. It's hard to say exactly what it is and where it comes from. Even creative people have a difficult time when trying to explain how they get their ideas. They may know intuitively, but trying to describe their creative methods puts them into a situation that is something of a paradox – a certain degree of creativity is needed in order to describe creativity.

The dictionary definition of creating is 'to originate; to bring into being from nothing'. Scientists may differ with the statement that something can come from nothing, but most agree that the concept of novelty plays an important role in creativity. Instead of claiming that a creative thought or idea arises 'out of nothing', researchers tend

ideas generation

to define creative thinking as the combining of previous ideas into new and interesting combinations. This may be a somewhat limited view, but it allows a more objective analysis and is the basis of many psychometric tests for creativity.

Creativity is often associated with 'right-brain' thinking. This refers to the discovery that the right and left hemispheres of the brain are specialised for different kinds of thought. In a right-handed person, the left hemisphere is associated with language, logic and analytical thinking, while the right is associated with visualisation and more conceptual, holistic thinking and is often considered the source of the imagination. The two hemispheres communicate with each other through a structure called the corpus callosum.

While the physical distinction between the hemispheres is real, recent research has make it clear that the functions of the two hemispheres are not so easily separated. For instance, while the main areas involved in using language are located in the left hemisphere, damage to the right hemisphere can affect some aspects of speech. Specifically, people with damage to the right frontal cortex don't use expressive inflections in their voice; they speak in a flat monotone whether happy or sad. Also, people with lesions at the back of the right hemisphere are unable to recognise such expressiveness in the speech of others. They can understand the words, but they aren't able to use the full range of expression available in human speech. Observations such as these suggest that both hemisphere of the brain are involved in complex processes such as using and understanding language. It is likely that creativity is also a 'global' process that uses many parts of the brain. In addition to the cerebral cortex, areas crucial to learning, memory, and emotions are probably important in creativity also.

Creative genius has been associated with madness since ancient times, and there are many examples of creative individuals that have suffered from mental illness – Vincent Van Gogh and Edgar Allan Poe come immediately to mind. While relationships between creativity and schizophrenia, psychosis, manic depression and attention deficit disorder have been suggested, no causal relationship has been proven, and it is important to remember that many people with mental illness are not particularly creative, and also there are many very creative people who are not mentally ill. Ongoing research in brain function in both mentally ill and 'normal' individuals will help elucidate any connection between mental illness and creativity.

The concepts of intelligence and genius are often associated with creativity and studies have shown that highly creative people are usually considered highly intelligent by common standards. However, a person with a high IQ does not necessarily exhibit a high level of creativity. In a famous study conducted early in this century, researchers followed 1500 children with high IQs (above 140). None of these children grew up to exhibit the levels of creativity commonly associated with genius. This suggests that there are indeed differences in the way that creative people think, and the convergent, analytic modes of thinking commonly measured by intelligence tests may be important for creative thought, but are not sufficient in themselves.

Originality is regarded as one of the key aspects of creativity, and one characteristic of creative people is their ability to think divergently, that is, to include analogies or combinations of ideas that may not be readily apparent,

ideas generation

may on the surface appear strange or without sense but open up possibilities that were previously overlooked. It is the uniqueness or oddness of these combinations that can give a truly creative act such a surprising character. If you think about Shakespeare's 'sweet sorrow' of parting, this is an odd mix of words that seems to evoke an amazing reaction in an audience. This is also a less than obvious combination of words that, when used together in this way, evoke something different from either word used alone.

While combining concepts in new and interesting ways is a major aspect of creativity, other important processes are involved. One related process is conceptual expansion. This term refers to the reworking of old, established ideas and forms into novel creations. An example is a composer using his knowledge of established musical form to compose an original piece. Other types of creative thinking could include the use of metaphor and analogy in developing novel ways of expressing or describing ideas. Existing knowledge also appears to play an important role in creativity by supplying a reserve of ideas and concepts that can be used as staring points in processes such as conceptual combination and expansion. This list of processes is far from complete, and there are many varying theories about and definitions of, the nature of creativity.

In addition to the processes already mentioned, researchers are also looking into many other factors that influence creativity, such as motivation, conceptual complexity and social value – for instance, what influence does society's acceptance or rejection of a creative act have on an individual's creativity?

One practical benefit of understanding how the creative process works is the development of methods to help people enhance their own creative thinking. Many different methods have been suggested, such as practising visualisation, keeping a written journal and practising creative associations (such as thinking of new uses for everyday items). Evidence has suggested that creativity may be inspired by the complexity of a situation, implying that continued learning could enhance creativity. There is also evidence that aerobic exercise helps enhance creativity – one recent study showed that people performed better on a creativity test if they exercised before taking the test. There are many possibilities for someone looking to increase their creative activity and each person will have to try out different techniques to find what will work for them. The experimentation itself can be a creative process and is a good way for a person to start expanding his or her creativity.

Thinking Creatively

Creativity is something that we all like to acknowledge as part of our own personalities; we pride ourselves on our cooking or home decorating, or we have secret ambitious to write a novel in retirement – all opportunities to be a little more creative than our normal routines allow.

So why does creativity appeal to us so much and why should we want to nurture it in ourselves? One of the secrets lies in the paragraph above – in the phrase 'write a novel'.

Novelty, the quality of being fresh and original, is at the centre of what it means to be creative. In its purest form it means bringing something into being where there

ideas generation

was nothing before. The skills needed for logical thinking and practical problem solving help us meet the challenges of daily living in a routine. But most of us would like to think that from time to time, we could transcend the familiar routines of practical organisation. Creative thinking involves imagination as well as intellect, it means leapfrogging beyond the professional, mechanical or academic solution, ultimately reaching a new kind of solution where there was no obvious answer before. In the most outstanding cases we are often overwhelmed by the simplicity of the idea as well as by its sheer innovation.

This ability to make an imaginative leap beyond the obvious characterises most of the major achievement in science and the arts throughout the ages. Above all, what makes the achievements stand out is that they break new ground. Bringing a creative dimension to problem-solving, then, may mean taking more risks, following guesses and estimates, testing and modifying possible solutions, bringing together the available information to form new relationships. If we had to make a very rough distinction between logical problem-solving and problem-solving with a creative approach, we might think of the logical solutions as the product of convergent thinking, an attempt to focus all the factors into one straight line leading directly to an answer; the creative solution would then be the product of divergent thinking, an attempt to find a solution that fits all the requirements, but which is quite far away from the obvious place to look.

What drives people to make use of their creative faculties? Creativity involves sustained and rigorous effort and most of us are quite resistant to unnecessary exertion. For many the motivation is the sheer love of inventing, of making new and interesting things. Others feel the desire to improve something, especially when it is for their own benefit or for the benefit of others close to them. Related to this is the powerful motivation of practical need. For others an incentive is financial gain, the opportunity to make their fortune by cornering the market with the most outstanding product in any particular field. Prestige is a high motivator too, bringing with it the possibility that your name might become a household word or a common entry in reference books. Finally, many are motivated by altruistic reasons – the desire to make something better or easier for other people – and their success is their own reward.

The idea that a brilliantly creative thought will suddenly come to you in a flash of inspiration is, sadly, an unrealistic one. Most ideas or solutions are the product of time, experimentation and other rejected thoughts; they are the result of a mixture of factors that have been fermenting in the brain for some time before they ever formulate into a clear idea.

So how does the brain think?
Experts have identified two basic patterns in human thinking. In the first the rational approach dominates, in the second it is the intuitive, creative, non-logical approach, and other states of consciousness take a part. Different experts have come up with a variety of names for the two patterns. Edward de Bono called them suparational thinking, intellectual and irrational or emotional thinking, or learning by authority and learning creatively. Whatever the name, we might think of these approaches as the two arms of intelligence, the first being logical and rational, and the second being your creative intelligence.

ideas generation

Some psychologists believe that, while both processes are needed for creative thinking, they cannot operate at the same time and that it is possible to develop training techniques, particularly for children, that call into play whichever kind of thinking would be most useful in any given situation. Although some people prefer to learn in creative ways, by exploring, manipulating, questioning or experimenting, and will respond badly to a rigid structure, there is much evidence to show that others respond better to a structured environment. On the whole, teachers will agree with this and add that it is more economical to learn by authority. It does seem, however, that people's preference for methods of learning and thinking can be altered, and that they can be trained to approach a problem in a way that is best suited to their lives and characters, possibly in as little as six to ten weeks.

Teaching the Brain

Each cerebral hemisphere of the brain – the left verbal-logical side and the right non-verbal holistic side – has its own part to play in working out the solution to a problem. During a period of incubation the conclusions produced by each hemisphere (and the rest of the brain) are combined to produce a whole, complete answer.

In order to achieve the maximum benefit from this incubation process, experts suggest that problems should be approached in three stages. The first arouses the interest of the brain and encourages the response of wanting to find a solution. In the second stage a person becomes more deeply involved in the problem and starts to look for solutions. In the final stage, thought processes are kept alive for as long as possible, so increasing the chances of successful creative thought through incubation.

4 Thinking the unthinkable

Creative Learning
Experts have learned a great deal about alternative approaches to learning by studying the behaviour of pre-school children. Left to their own devices children learn by experimenting, manipulating and rearranging objects, singing, dancing and storytelling. At times this kind of learning is rapid and spontaneous, at other times the response of the children is more measured or slower. When they are learning in creative ways young children have amazingly long attention spans, they do not like to skip from one activity to another, and if interrupted they like to go back to the absorbing activity. Highly creative children have surprisingly capacity for organising things, and will return many times to familiar tasks or sequences to look at them in different ways and in greater depth.

Enhancing Creativity
Once the most essential elements of creative thinking have been established, it is up to each of us to try and use these newly identified skills to improve our own creativity, not only in terms of producing the next bestseller or artistic masterpiece, but simply in the way we approach our own lives and the problems that we need to overcome. The essence of creative thought lies in clearly identifying the problem, in using original approaches to come up with as many solutions as possible, keeping your mind open to new ideas and making successful and innovative choices about the options. When these basic steps are combined with other creative techniques such as visualisation, fantasy, the use of movement and sound, humour, and putting things in perspective and in context, the chances of coming up with a satisfactory and satisfying answer to everyday problems is greatly increased.

ideas generation

If, for instance, you have a colleague at work whom you find so irritating that it is affecting your state of mind both at work and at home, what is the best way of dealing with the situation? The first step is to identify clearly what the problem is. Is it a conflict of characters? Is it something that you are doing that is provoking their outburst? Is it directed at you or everyone in the office? Whichever it is will determine the possible solutions – to snap back at them, to totally ignore them, to leave the job, or to complain to someone else, for example.

Leaving emotions (anger, irritation, etc) to one side, the situation may seem a bit different. Treated with humour, it might become clear that this person who is doing their best to make life difficult does not need to affect your working life, and especially not your home life. Making positive, friendly moves toward them, no matter how galling, might undermine their line of attack.

Whatever the final solution, however, stepping back and looking at any situation in a detached frame of mind will usually bring even the largest or most complex problem back into perspective.

Improving your Creative Potential

The following list may help to enhance your creative thinking skills; they suggest adjustments to personality and different attitudes, which might assist your creativity.

- Do not be afraid to pursue an interest with intensity; most people do best in what they enjoy most.
- Know, understand and develop your greatest strengths.
- Free yourself from the expectations of others and avoid the restrictions they impose.

4 Thinking the unthinkable

- Follow your own instincts and lead your own life so that you can make the most of your gifts.
- Find a teacher or mentor whose opinion you respect and who can make useful suggestions.
- Do not try to do everything or to be an all-rounder.
- Try not to waste creative energy where you have no real interest.

Developing Creativity

The following are just a few of the ways that you can encourage the development of creative thinking skills in yourself and in even very young children:

- Provide toys, books and other materials that will encourage creative thinking and creative play.
- Provide some unstructured play materials (such as blocks, clay and paint) to help children create their own ideas and develop an imagination.
- Help children to 'pretend' by inventing the situation and saying to the child, "I wonder what would happen if...?" Try to stretch your child's imagination.
- Help children to see that there are always alternative answers to a problem. Encourage them to look for other situations.
- Allow time for thinking and daydreaming.
- Encourage children to record their ideas by drawing them or by telling their ideas to adults or older children. Drawing a problem is an excellent way to solve it creatively.
- Give children's ideas some concrete encouragement, by displaying drawings or using their designs on clothes, china, etc.

ideas generation

- Don't tamper with or 'improve' children's songs, poems, pictures, etc.
- Encourage unusual or different ways of looking at a subject.
- Help children to solve their problems within the family in a constructive way.
- Rather than suppressing disruptive or destructive behaviour, try to turn it into positive energy.

What are Creative Thinking Skills?

- Defining the problem – identifying a need.
- Being able to see different aspects, versions and points of view.
- Approaching the situation in an original way.
- Highlighting the most important elements.
- Elaborating on specific features.
- Keeping an open mind at every stage.
- Putting ideas into context.
- Being aware of and listening to your emotions.
- Combining and synthesising ideas from different areas.
- Visualising richly and colourfully.
- Fantasising.
- Using movement and sound.
- Looking at things from a different perspective.
- Extending boundaries.
- Being humorous.

By making conscious efforts to develop these skills, creative people express themselves in a variety of ways, including music, science, art and literature.

Left Versus the Right Hemisphere of the Brain

If the left hemisphere of your brain is dominant, you:

- Tend to be conforming
- Prefer structured assignments
- Like systems and structure
- Like to solve problems logically
- Like order and cohesion
- Like facts

If the right hemisphere of your brain is dominant, you:

- Tend to be non-conforming
- Prefer open-ended assignments
- Like to discover through exploration
- Like to use intuition
- Like to be inventive
- Don't need as much order
- Like to use your imagination

How do I know I'm creative?

The prevailing mythology has it that creativity is the exclusive domain of artists, scientists and inventors – a giftedness not available to ordinary people going about the business of daily life. Partly as a result, ordinary people often hold the creative person in awe, believing that they are somehow a genius. It's either George Lucas or nothing.

Creativity in its fullest sense involves both generating an idea and manifesting it – making something happen as a result. To strengthen creative ability, you need to apply the idea in some form that enables both the experience itself and your own and others' reaction to reinforce your performance. As you and others applaud your creative endeavours, you are likely to become more creative.

Defining creativity to include application throws the whole subject into a different light, because:

- While ideas can come in seconds, application can take days, years or even a lifetime to realise.
- While ideas can come out of only one quadrant, application ultimately calls on specialised mental capabilities in all four quadrants of the brain.
- While ideas can arrive in a single flash, application necessarily involves a process consisting of several distinct phases.

What can I do to increase my creativity?

The simplest answer of all, based on the power of our subconscious is, "Take a walk." How many ideas have you had while you were jogging, walking, gardening, washing the dishes or driving? Our subconscious mind is constantly processing the ideas and stimuli received consciously. A useful technique is to actively work on a problem before going to sleep, allowing the subconscious to take over. Review any ideas when you awake, and make sure you have a pad and pen by your bed to record your ideas.

A person's creativity is often influenced by their viewpoint on creativity. As soon as we try to create, i.e. 'to do it', we start controlling. We have to learn to loosen control, to let the mind be.

Creativity is like a cat chasing its tail. In the act of creating or in solving problems in creative ways we often go round and round in endless circles wanting to pounce on an idea. Sometimes the answer or solution is right before our eyes but we can't see it. In order to find the solution, find the missing piece, solve the problem, we need to just look at something familiar in a new and different way.

Levels of Creativity
The first three levels of creativity can be attained by anyone with motivation and persistence. The last two may be unattainable to all but the inspired or the naturally creative genius.

1. **Primitive and intuitive expression:** The first level incorporates the primitive and intuitive expression found in children and in adults who have not been trained in creativity. There is an innocent quality to primitive creativity, but also directness and sensitivity. The naïve ideas generator creates for the joy of it.
2. **Academic and technical level:** The second level of creativity is the academic and technical level. At this level the person learns skills and techniques, developing a proficiency that allows creative expression in myriad ways.
3. **Inventive level:** Many people experiment with their creativity, exploring different ways of using familiar tools and mediums. This heralds the level of invention. Breaking rules is the order of the day, challenging the boundaries of academic tradition, becoming increasingly adventurous and experimental. Inventors use academic tradition and skills as a stepping-stone into new frontiers.
4. **Innovative level:** At the level of innovation the artist, writer, musician, inventor, thinker is more

ideas generation

original. Materials and methods that are out of the ordinary are introduced. Now the creator breaks the boundaries. The academic or inspirational foundation remains as a substructure of unconscious thought guiding these creative efforts.
5. **Genius level**: The fifth level of creativity is characterised as genius. There are individuals whose ideas and accomplishments in art and science defy explanation. Genius is arguably the one level that is unexplainable and perhaps unattainable, something that an individual is born with.

Characteristics of highly creative individuals
Highly creative individuals may:

- Display a great deal of curiosity about many things; constantly ask questions about anything and everything; have broad interests in many unrelated areas; devise collections based on unusual things and interests.
- Generate a large number of ideas or solutions to problems and questions; offer unusual ('way out'), unique, clever responses.
- Be uninhibited in expressions of opinion; sometimes radical and spirited in disagreement; be unusually tenacious or persistent – fixating on an idea or project.
- Be willing to take risks, be described as high risk-takers, or adventurous, or speculative.
- Display a good deal of intellectual playfulness; frequently be caught fantasising, daydreaming or imagining. Often wonder out loud, saying,

"I wonder what would happen if..." or, " What if we change..." Manipulate ideas by easily changing, elaborating, adapting, improving, or modifying the original idea or the ideas of others. Often improves the conceptual frame works of institutions, objects, and systems.
- Display a keen sense of humour in situations that may not appear to be humorous to others. Sometimes their humour may appear bizarre, inappropriate, and irreverent to others.
- Exhibit heightened emotional sensitivity. May be not only sensitive to beauty but visibly moved by aesthetic experiences.
- Often be perceived as nonconforming; accept disordered or chaotic environments or situations; frequently not be interested in details, be described as individuals or do not fear being classified as 'different'.
- Criticise constructively, and be unwilling to accept authoritarian pronouncements without overly critical self-examination.

Forms of Creative Inspiration

There are many things that inspire creative acts. Inspiration is an important part of the creative process. Here are some of the documented historical examples of sources of inspiration.

- *Triggers and flashes:* Nature is often a primary source for creative production, as are common things that surround our lives – a sunset, a mountain, a verse of a song, a certain phrase, a child's smile.

ideas generation

- ***Being in love:*** being out of love; tormented by rejected love. Centuries of love poems testify to this.
- ***Desperation:*** Office worker Betty Nesmith, mother of Mike Nesmith of the 1960s Monkees pop group, was a divorcee with three children to support. She had a job in a typing pool, but was not a good typist, and was afraid she would be fired, which would be disastrous. So she invented Liquid Paper, a means of concealing her typing mistakes.

5

Incorporating consumer trends into the ideas process

How trends can help you develop timely ideas.

Inside the offices of some of the most creative and well-known film studios around the world sits a curious sign: 'If you can't sell it – don't make it'. Not surprisingly, many from independent film communities scoff at such an attempt to 'commercialise' the integrity of a film. They will say that creativity is a personal expression and should therefore not involve the audience until well after the creative process has been completed. But is this truly the case? Was it ever the case? After all, even Mozart wrote specifically for an audience.

In a world where dividing lines are fast disappearing and it is getting much harder to judge the difference between art, creativity, advertising, originality, the good and the just plain old bad, the question is: How should we approach the role of audiences or 'markets' when developing or even generating ideas? Even the definitions

ideas generation

have undergone marked changes over the last ten years. What is art? What is creativity? What is advertising? What is originality? While these questions are best left to the philosophers among us, as original thinkers we do have to answer two questions:

- Where does an idea begin and where does it end?
- At which point does an idea belong to an audience or market?

We often get asked our views on the nature of the divide between true originality and commercially motivated creativity. Or more frequently these days, we get asked whether there will be a divide in the future at all. Our views are simply this: art in its purest form resides completely outside of the commercial realm. To create art is a pursuit of self-expression that does not depend on the whims of a target market. Artists don't do what they do for anyone else, they primarily do it for themselves. That is not to say however that artists live in a vacuum (all of the artists we know or have interviewed in the past cannot survive without the sense of appreciation that goes with the process of pleasing an audience). What is does say is something about the purity of artistic motivation. The great artists don't seem to have a choice in the matter. Their entire existence is all a matter of purity and a commitment to the integrity of the work. Jeff Buckley, one of the most original musical artists of the late twentieth century, put it best when he said:

"There is much music I will never let the public see – I don't write for Sony, I write for the people I see driving down the highway listening to music with tears streaming down their faces."

The simultaneous commitment to an audience, the self and the work is the hallmark of a great artist.

However, that said, we above all believe in originality over creativity or art. Originality and art are not one and the same in our minds. Originality, in our opinion, should be viewed as a truth that judges the quality of our thinking and ideas. There is nothing worse than derivative art or derivative creativity.

So it therefore makes sense that in order to be constantly original, an intimate understanding of people and a constantly outward-looking perspective is crucial. You at least must have a good idea of what has been done before in order to create something totally new. This is the point at which social trends analysis starts to become a tool for ideas generation.

Ideas in the real world
There is a long road between an idea for a movie and a movie that actually makes it to the big screen. The road is fraught with compromises, many of which most people would not even contemplate.

As you have probably noticed by now, we refer often to the creation of movies for ease of example. This is due to the ubiquitous nature of film and the fact that almost everyone has an idea for a movie tucked in a bottom drawer somewhere.

One of the most sobering things to watch is a test screening of a film – particularly one where the director seems to have lost some of the creative control over the process. A test screening is where a studio will have an audience watch a rough edit of the film in order to understand how they felt about aspects of the story itself. In some cases, endings to movies have been changed

ideas generation

because a test audience reacted negatively to some element of the story. *Pretty Woman* had its ending changed after audiences reacted negatively to Richard Gere and Julia Roberts not living happily ever after. Many in the film business decry the use of test screenings. How is one able to please entire audiences all of the time? Shouldn't an original film be completed before it is seen by an audience? Or should a studio ensure that a film is going to do its job – entertain, engage or challenge large amounts of people by testing it first?

Certainly, both points of view can be right, depending on the amount of money at stake at the production stage. Money often sorts out the definitions between pure creativity and commercial creativity and in the movie business the stakes are high. If, for example, you happen to be James Cameron on the set of Titanic with the production budget tipping the US$100 million mark – you had better be prepared to be asked many questions about the potential of the film to make back the money invested. That will usually mean quite a number of test screenings at the very least.

If you are a painter however and you have devoted all of your personal time and money to a project, do not be prepared to answer to anyone concerning creative output. The fact of the matter is, if you are going to play with other people's money, you should be prepared to yield some percentage of the creative control you have over your work. Ideas need money somewhere along the line. Unfortunately it can't be avoided. It must also be said that Australians on the whole seem to be 'capital shy' when it comes to sacrificing levels of ownership in order to raise money to develop ideas. When it comes to raising capital, it is just a matter of ensuring that the money comes at

5 Incorporating consumer trends into the ideas process

a minimal price. There is nothing worse than expensive money!

The central question for the ideas generation process when it comes to the role of audiences and consumers has more to do with the differences between inward and outward motivations than with commercial versus non-commercial motivations. In other words, as a thinker, a writer, an entertainer, an inventor, a film-maker or a painter, how closely and regularly do you consider your audience during the creative process? How can this consideration help you to be constantly original? How can a focus on your audience help you at all? The saying goes that you should only need one good reason in life, so in terms of an audience focus, here it is: *If you can demonstrate a very articulate understanding of the evolution of your idea and how people will interact with it, you will have an increased chance of retaining creative control throughout the development process.*

Make no mistake, if you have a great idea (or even if you have an average idea), chances are that someone along the line is going to offer to buy the work or distribute the work for you. This is the first 'outing' of your idea in the real world and perhaps your first tangible evidence that you are any good at anything! If you are lucky enough to be a writer, industry standards usually ensure a level of fairness to negotiations. If, however, you have developed the world's first engine that runs on water, you had better get yourself the most expensive law firm in the Yellow Pages.

An initial approach from any potential purchaser or capital partner therefore often seems like a dream come true (especially when you have been working on a project in isolation for an extended period of time). But a

ideas generation

word of warning: Do not jump too fast toward the first opportunity. The ability to act independently in the ideas game is central to your success in constantly creating a new environment from which you can launch new ideas. It may also be central to the success of your original idea when you consider the fact that you may be the only person with the ability to bring the idea to its full potential. A great example of this is Jodie Foster's character in the film *Contact*. She finds herself in a situation where she has to constantly fight for the right to hold on to the leadership of her project and the only way she stays in the game is due to the intellectual 'inside runs' bestowed on her by her very wealthy sponsor. We certainly recommend you watch the film and focus on the sub-theme of the ownership of ideas.

Our advice to those who get approaches from companies early in the game who are very eager to buy 'a piece' of your idea is simply this: Be very careful from whom you accept help when it comes to your ideas and, as stated previously, be very careful who you speak to and what you put on your personal home page or Web site. In these cases knowledge, and lots of it, is the best protection mechanism for you as you go forward. Understanding your audience via trends analysis will put you in a better position to defend your place as the rightful leader of the development team.

Do not be too proud to investigate in a little understanding of how the 'average' person lives their life! We know that once you have reached the dizzy heights of ideas genius you will cut yourself off from the common man (and woman) but do not be too quick to do so. Always be motivated by the fact that your idea will affect and touch people.

5 Incorporating consumer trends into the ideas process

We raise these issues of motivation at the beginning of this chapter for very specific reasons:

- Understanding where your natural tendency lies on the issue of inward versus outward motivation is the key to understanding the use of trends.
- Identifying your opinion on the role of an audience or the end-user of an idea in the development of the idea itself is also key.
- Understanding and plotting where an idea or a creative expression ends and the audience begins will also affect your views on the use of trends data in assisting the original thought process.

Now that we have legitimised the role of 'punters' in the ideas generation process, let's move on to legitimising the role of trends analysis.

The world around us

Understanding the forces that are motivating people in different parts of the world is a foundation of creativity and original thought.

While the trends referred to in this chapter generally apply to developed Western cultures, we are currently developing techniques that allow our research teams to understand how the imagery from Western cultures is mixing with the local culture. We have found that tracking trends in eastern European and Asian countries is trickier than tracking Western trends. In our Asian trend tracking we usually employ a local team to prepare a report on the trajectory of the culture over the last twenty years. This report gives us a roadmap of how the culture has developed over the last few decades and some

ideas generation

insight into how it might look (as a culture) in ten or twenty years time. This gives us a starting point.

In the West, spotting trends has become a very popular corporate pursuit over the last couple of years, with several companies specialising in the practice in Australia, the US and the UK. The value of adding trends analysis to the business planning process is reasonably obvious and although the discipline has been in existence since 1965, Australian companies are only now starting to realise that a deeper understanding of social trends (in the more formal guise of social forecasting) will ultimately yield more fruitful research and development within any organisation.

The cutting edge of the practice, however, lies in its ability both to create new ideas and to measure the scope and importance of existing ones. In this chapter we will attempt to simplify the process by leaving out many of the statistical and mathematical methods used to decode trends information. Instead, we will attempt to give you a foundation of knowledge that will allow you to develop your own keen sense of smell when it comes to spotting societal trends – which should be enough to help you create more ideas than you could possibly transform into reality in one single lifetime!

Spotting the horizon

Understanding where consumers are moving, both in terms of their consumption patterns but more importantly in terms of their motivational cycles, is one of the most fertile areas we have discovered in constantly generating new ideas. People tend to move in unique ways, both as individuals and as populations, as they grapple with progress, relationships, career and parenting. New tech-

5 Incorporating consumer trends into the ideas process

nologies come and go, political leaders and ideologies come and go but one thing remains constant throughout: the human ability to regenerate.

Regeneration, whether it is the regeneration of the human body or the regenerative ability of cultures and communities to rebuild, is the nature of the human spirit. With regeneration comes original and creative thinking. With necessity comes invention. As the world moves forward, there is great value in pre-empting the needs, desires and motivations of people who are on the journey. The greatest gift the practice offers is the genuine experience of putting yourself in other people's shoes, because in order to forecast where societal trends are going you must first know thoroughly the people who make up that society. Perspective is one of the great feats the mind can accomplish and it is a practice we encourage you to learn to control at will. Think of trends as the creative cycles within a developed society that keep the population moving.

Thinking ahead to the end user or the audience for an idea can very much be part of the creative process. Appreciating the fact that every time someone uses or experiences your idea they are actually extending the idea itself will redefine how you imagine your idea as a finished product. While we would never encourage a creative person to think about how to sell a work before contemplating it – money has little to do with the nature of original thought – we would, however, recommend that people resign themselves to the fact that originality is not owned by any one individual – it is the human condition. Once people realise and accept this, they usually find new respect for the people who must bring an idea into the real world – the audience. There is nothing

103

ideas generation

worse than sitting at a rock concert where the performer seems totally self-absorbed and oblivious to the audience! Never again place yourself 'above' your audience.

True creativity and originality come with a certain humility and humanity. Those who genuinely understand where ideas come from and what makes them real tend to get to enjoy very long careers in their chosen field. True creators understand that they are the servants of those whom their ideas affect. George Lucas understands it. Paul McCartney understands it. Madonna understands it!

The other truly creative question is whether an idea is actually ever finished. Does a film evolve each time it is viewed? Does an artwork take a new perspective with every new set of eyes? Does a novel hold new promise upon a second reading? Most importantly, is the idea completed only when it is absorbed by an audience?

To understand that ideas have a life of their own is to understand the entire contents of this book. You never own your ideas (if anything, they own you). They change of their own accord, which is why this entire book is devoted to systems that help you manage and parent the growth and development of ideas.

It is a key responsibility of creators to understand, project and predict the environment in which ideas will be expected to grow. Just as a farmer must plant the right crop in the right location, understanding the exact needs of his or her seed, so too an inventor must understand where his or her invention is best suited to growing – before the idea is planted.

So when and how does an idea get planted we hear you ask? Here is the next most important point: an idea is planted as soon as you open your mouth to someone about it.

5 Incorporating consumer trends into the ideas process

We cannot stress enough how important it is that you refrain from speaking about your ideas. Showing people an idea is very different from speaking about one. Always ensure that you breathe life into your ideas by creating tangible prototypes before you speak to anyone. It's exactly the same as having a baby for the first time. People around you are experts on what is best for the child and new parents tend to listen to others for the first couple of weeks, until they understand and learn to listen to their intuition; then they know they have the necessary skills embedded into their psyche.

Spawning ideas comes even more naturally to us than spawning children. It is our key survival mechanism as a species. How do you think we have survived so long stuck out in the middle of a desolate solar system all on our own?

So by now you get the idea that ideas are a life form. So let us look at some techniques that we have developed that, on the one hand, assist in the environmental assessment for each idea, and on the other hand, help create new ideas from scratch.

What are trends?

Trends are simply the social and economic lifecycles that pulse through a society. They are nature's influence and steadying hand on the human world.

The world of nature is made up of cycles. The moon waxes and wanes, the tide comes in and the tide goes out. Rivers flow to the ocean, birds in the northern hemisphere fly south for the winter then return. The delicate balance of any ecosystem is held together by the cyclical influence of nature. Without these cycles, nature grows stagnant and dies. One of the greatest mistakes that

ideas generation

mankind has made in the past is to think that we are beyond the laws of nature. We are not.

Trends make up the micro-fabric of mankind's natural cycles. You will already be aware of many of them – economic trends, fashion trends, musical trends and social trends, for example. But social analysts are in the business of studying others – such as motivational trends – that you may not have heard of before.

Trends analysis and social forecasting are surprisingly creative and insightful techniques. They often yield an understanding of the 'grain' that is running through a society. The science of identifying and tracking trends relies on a statistical grouping method called *cluster analysis*, which provides a tool to identify and group social themes. The value of this method lies in its ability to group social themes that have not been grouped before. This technique also relies on 'what if' scenario planning to fill in the gaps between where hard evidence stops and assumptions begin.

Often, we will also mix together statistics that are usually quoted very separately. Retail sales and box office figures when put together will often create an insight into the overall mood of a community.

Trends Analysis Case Study

Trends analysis often yields many new insights and ideas. Two years ago Pophouse was conducting a study into food and restaurant trends in the US. We were particularly interested in the rise of indulgence and fatty foods on many menus in exclusive Los Angeles restaurants. Out initial thoughts led us to believe that these new main courses were simply representative of the fact that when the economy gets fat with cash, people tend to want to

5 Incorporating consumer trends into the ideas process

get fat with food. We couldn't have been further from the truth. Apart from the fact that the project meant we ate at some of the best restaurants in the US (a tough job, but someone's gotta do it!), we stumbled upon a mix of social themes that had not run in parallel before. When we found that some of the most elegant establishments were actually serving chicken with the skin on, we knew we were on to something.

The project involved interviews with the 100 most innovative chefs in Los Angeles, San Francisco, Seattle, Portland and New York. This is the hard slog fieldwork required within every project to establish the collective thoughts of opinion leaders in a particular field. The results of these interviews were surprisingly similar, with most of the chefs reporting that large, whole foods were making an incredible resurgence at the expense of exotic dishes. The question that troubled us was: Did the chefs first listen and think of their customers or did they work in isolation and serve what they themselves had liked at another venue? Those of you who happen to know chefs will not be surprised to learn that we recorded hundreds of hours of conversation without really managing to get direct answers to this question. We did, however, learn that chefs mixed art and originality in their menus in order to please their diners.

But back to the mystery of the chicken with the skin on. What struck us as strange was that during times of high economic prosperity in the past, exotic foods had emerged as the most popular choice of exclusive restaurants. French cuisine, complicated presentation and minimalist quantity had all been the hallmarks of those who wanted to display the fact that they could pay huge amounts of money to be served a basically empty plate.

ideas generation

This change had not been lost on the chefs themselves:

"This rise in whole food consumption seems to stem from a sense that people are absolutely crazy and complicated in every other aspect of their lives," said Jason Van Wyckle, the owner of four restaurants in Los Angeles. *"I know that every generation has been busy in their time, but it would seem that these days, whilst people are busy, they still have the time to contemplate their belly buttons. Big whole food is definitely on the rise. Some of the other chefs I know actually put the source of the produce on the menu. They are treating food in the same way that we used to treat wine and that is, we value the integrity of the source."*

This is where the fun began for us. We already knew that consumers of information on the Internet and elsewhere were concerned that there was too much information too unreliably sourced. There was also a trend for people to search for dependable value in consumption of goods and services generally. After our initial round of fieldwork we were left with a couple of hypotheses.

- Could a shift in eating habits be a reaction to the sense of loss of control that people felt they had over their lives?
- Were people looking to regain their 'innocence' in a time of excess consumerism? Would the new definition of indulgence have an innocence to it that was not seen in the last economic boom?

We certainly felt we had enough anecdotal evidence to keep investigating further.

The first thing any good trendspotter will must do when he or she finds a new trend is to give it a name,

5 Incorporating consumer trends into the ideas process

preferably one journalists and advertising executives will pick up on. We gave our new trend a name: *Grinnocence*, capturing the mix of fun and innocence in the new trend towards indulgence. The Australian media picked up very quickly on this term with a number of major newspapers running feature stories on the work we had conducted.

The next stage of the project involved a brief from a US retail developer who was looking toward the launch of a new multi-retail complex and wanted to better understand the current definition of 'indulgence'. Should indulgence be presented in terms of purchases or in terms of time? Our response to them (via a lengthy report) was direct: *The simple things are the new indulgence and this presents a major market opportunity for several product categories including: Community newspapers, organic foods; movies and TV that focus on homespun tales and relationships; cafes; market gardening products; local vineyards and produce (to name a few).*

If a major retailer could capture the essence of 'grinnocence' in a mall or shopping centre environment, he would have a substantial new revenue stream on his hands. We knew that the logistics of our idea would present a problem, mainly because the consortium had already committed itself to a certain design. Luckily enough, their plans included a large open space that seemed to have no particular function.

The process of looking at the developer's needs on the one hand and the trends information we had generated on the other started in earnest. The way Pophouse works as a creative organisation is unique; we have a policy of never working with the same team twice, which tends to

ideas generation

ensure that we are always 'on a first date' in intellectual terms with each of the team members. The creative energy generated by meeting and working constantly with new people is something our organisation is totally addicted to, and the clients seem to love it. Effectively we form a new company for each and every project. We are blessed with a great variety of talented people who are willing to 'rent out' their brains for days at a time. These people come from an eclectic mix of professional backgrounds. On this particular retail development project we had a doctor, a music video director, a botanist, an unemployed teacher and a lawyer. As you can imagine, the results both in terms of value and volume of ideas generated at these creative sessions are extraordinary.

Part of our creative process usually includes an excursion or two. The theory is that we should keep moving our physical location in order to either break a deadlock or drill down further into the detail of an idea. In this instance we took a trip to upstate New York to look at some berry farms. The theme of our idea or our hunting ground, actually stemmed from the name of a recent Neil Young album 'Harvest Moon'. Someone had brought the album in to one of our brainstorming sessions for some unknown reason and it had infected us with an organic slant. In fact we all became so totally obsessed with the word 'harvest' that we thought we should head north and do some berry picking. Whilst we were enjoying the July sun and working in the fields (apart from breaking into spontaneous gospel song) we actually managed to all agree on the same idea. It was this: *Burn the concept of malls and resurrect the concept of the HARVEST!*

The idea actually sounded crazy enough to go with. Wouldn't it be wonderful to create a living field inside a

5 Incorporating consumer trends into the ideas process

mall that actually brought the country back into the city? Wasn't this the essence of the grinnocence trend? Back to the simple, earthy pleasures of life? Wasn't being able to drive up to a berry farm on a workday the ultimate indulgence?

We recommended the creation of 'market gardens' within the design of the mall, using the sunlight in the unused atrium area to grow a range of fruits and vegetables. The whole idea centred on the creation of place in the mall that was indulgent in terms of the *amount of time* the customers devoted to it. Our idea, inspired by the grinnocence trend, consisted of an environment that was fun, educational and organic.

Instead of devoting the centre of the mall to a dull atrium, our design included the construction of a living market garden of fruits and berries where people could come and 'harvest' their own produce. Parents could also teach their small children about the agricultural process at the 'organic food learning centre'. In the environment of genetically modified foods, this concept immediately caught the imagination of the senior executives at board level. We then approached a homeware manufacturer to design a 'market garden starters kit' that would assist people in setting up their own market gardens at home.

As you can see, once you hit on a social trend and investigate the themes and motivations beneath it, you find a pool of ideas and original thoughts. You also tend to have a much clearer picture of the types of new products and services that would suit new markets.

But most important of all, you generally create for yourself the basis of a very compelling argument as to why your idea will work. We are not too embarrassed to admit that had we not had the grinnocence data we

ideas generation

would not have stumbled on to the idea and we certainly would not have been able to convince the developers to back it.

So was the market garden built? In a twist of fate, the developers onsold their holdings to another firm who apparently still have the idea on the plans for 'phase two of the project'. See what we mean when we say that you have to be detached from your ideas? It is just too heartbreaking to watch a lost opportunity slip by under the weight of corporate politics!

When ideas are put on the back-burner you realise the value of detailed contracts between yourself and clients. This is a good case in point because the new developer actually inherited the agreement we had with the previous developer. This means that we receive payment on a royalty basis if the project goes ahead, with or without our involvement. We also went to the trouble of registering the trademark for the indoor market garden concept which further protected our intellectual property.

If your organisation is a small one, you must ensure you have as much money as possible available for trademarks, registrations and general legal costs.

Trends to watch over the next five years

While many commentators and 'trend-trackers' speak in broad motherhood statements without ever really producing anything concrete in terms of ideas for new products or services, this should not discourage your use of trends data. There are some obvious trends that you should keep an eye on and possibly mine for new ideas or package as evidence to support an existing idea. Remember that these can be tracked via the newspapers or from a variety of free media on the Internet.

5 Incorporating consumer trends into the ideas process

Here are some examples of the social and economic trends we are tracking at the moment.

Localism
Basically, this trend is a direct reaction to globalism, the Internet and the sense that life is becoming more dangerous. Local communities are springing up in all major cites. Certainly many films in production at the moment focus on a local community and the trials and tribulations within it. Urban landscapes are also being modified by this trend, particularly in major capital cities, as people attempt to live outside the urban area whilst still obtaining work there. In Melbourne, while conducting a trends audit for a developer in 1999, we found that as many as 33 per cent of professionals were hoping to sell their suburban residences and buy two replacement residences — an apartment in the city and a home in the outer regions such as the Dandenongs. Products and services that promote or exude a local sentiment will find new markets. We expect this trend to peak within the next three years.

Humble Pie
The twentieth century can be characterised in many ways but it will definitely be remembered as the age of celebrity. Starting with the birth of Hollywood in the early 1900s, peaking with the launch of television in the 1950s and becoming entrenched in the multimedia world of the early 1990s, celebrities have played a major role in defining the values and aspirations of millions of people around the world. Marilyn Monroe, Elvis Presley, Michael Jackson, Audrey Hepburn and Princess Diana will forever be remembered as icons of the twentieth century who realised the potential (negative and positive) of celebrity.

ideas generation

But something happened in 1998 that could signal the end of the reign of celebrity. A maverick Internet site called The Drudge Report started to circulate information regarding the president of the United States, Bill Clinton, and an intern named Monica Lewinsky. Their affair became the fodder of Internet sites across the globe and suddenly the power of celebrity (which has always been founded in the power and reach of the electronic media) started to falter. Celebrities started to lose their appeal to the middle class as value systems started to shift (mainly due to the fact that the new economy began to raise entrepreneurs to celebrity stakes of a different kind). The essential mystery of the celebrity, fostered but not exposed by the then media, was dissolved by more information. Celebrity is not as mysterious as it once was. Witness the dramatic decline in weekly magazines, which used to be filled with pictures of celebrities in all sorts of situations. One of the primary reasons for their falling popularity is the fact that technology has succeeded in lifting the veil and mystery from the media, the engine that creates celebrity. Young school kids are able to produce all sorts of media-related products from their own desktop computers – e-zines, short films and Web pages just to name a few. Once the mystery goes, so does the leverage.

You may have noticed that the smartest celebrities (who genuinely treat themselves as household brands) have begun to appear in public dressed casually and without the usual entourage of staff. We call this trend the Humble Pie movement. Many of these celebrities are repositioning themselves as community spokespeople (Denzel Washington, Pierce Brosnan and Jewel to name a few), where they actively get involved in causes. This is very different from the Live Aid fever that gripped the rock movement in the 1980s. In fact, the Creative Artists Agency in the US recently announced the launch of a special service for their celebrity clients: 'cause management'. That is, the appointment of a manager to handle the growing number of requests flooding in from community groups and charities so that their clients might take on the 'right' causes.

Humility as a strategy is very much an extension of the community trends flowing through the developed cultures of the world. If it is your job to come up with ideas on how to promote and position a company in the market place you would do well to investigate this trend in depth. Companies that take their community responsibilities seriously will be the ones to develop great brands in the new millennium. Brands like Benetton, The Body Shop and Virgin have been surfing the undercurrent of this trend almost on their own for many years.

It always amazes us that so many organisations fail to recognise a theory espoused by many of the great American futurists – the triple bottom line. That is, the responsibility a corporation has to the community, the environment and the shareholders. Once a company acts with genuine humility (and that means a strategy founded in the belief that the company's main role is to serve the community), great brands can be created overnight.

If you need proof of the effectiveness of this strategy, ask one of the Qantas shareholders in Australia who watched the capitalisation of the airline crash almost $1 billion because Richard Branson announced he was going to launch Virgin Airways on a foundation of affordable fares for all.

Psychological Testing

A clean bill of psychological health looks like becoming an obsession for people in the developed nations over the next five years. We are expecting to see a steep rise in the number of personality tests available in the market. Employers want to be sure they are employing the 'right' person for the job and someone who is psychologically stable.

Personality testing has quite a long history. The first test was the Woodworth Personal Data Sheet which first appeared in 1918 and was designed to help the US army screen out recruits who might be susceptible to shell shock. One of the most widely used tests by employers is called the Thematic Apperception Test or TAT, while others have included the Rorschach inkblot and the Minnesota Multiphasic Personality Inventory (MMPI).

Many in the psychological fraternity believe that personality tests will be as important as medical tests in the near future. Increasingly, employers are looking for greater certainty when choosing employees and the psychological assessment industry is currently worth around US$400 million.

It sounds Orwellian, doesn't it? The fact that your psychological disposition may well be a matter of public record in the future? Obviously, screening applicants for some jobs, airline pilots for example, requires in-depth physical and emotional assessment. But what about a psychological test that determines the suitability of your girlfriend or boyfriend? Some of these types of tests are already appearing on the Internet as 'scenario tests', allowing people to observe potential partners in a controlled situation so his or her personality type may be ascertained under pressure.

The psychological testing trend is the final instalment of the self-improvement trend of the late 1980s and early 1990s. Self-proclaimed gurus like Anthony Robbins popularised the pursuit of self-focus without guilt; now psychology is designing and profiting from an increased use of personality assessment by corporations around the globe.

The value in tracking this trend lies in the fact that it yields a substantial amount of information and insight concerning how people will value themselves in the future. Make no mistake. The market for self-assessment tools and self-development techniques is big and getting bigger. How many ideas can you generate that will service this demand?

Other Trends We are Currently Tracking

Our primary trend-tracking engine is called the Pophouse 'social census', a poll we conduct on a quarterly basis with 2500 Australians. It acts as a kind of open diary, where panellists submit their answers to a series of questions on the future.

The trends that we are tracking over the course of 2000 include:

- The redefinition of community
- The wired home
- Radio Online
- Student activism
- Leadership
- The multiple futures of racism
- Technology forecasting
- New social paradigms of the third millennium
- Smorgasboard spirituality

ideas generation

Further information on the Pophouse Social Census can be found at www.pophouse.com.au

6

The 21 Step Ideas Production Line: S.I.m.P.L.e. Steps 1 to 7

Generating thousands of ideas for yourself, your business and your future.
Doubling your failure rate. Avoiding linear thought by making unexpected connections. Creating a context for divergent thinking.

We have deliberately chosen to use the words 'production line'. Why? Because most people treat ideas as if they're eggshells – they become too afraid to touch them, to criticise them, to challenge them and finally to change them.

At Pophouse we believe that ideas should only be given the respect they deserve when they become reality, so we try not to be too precious with our ideas. Using the phrase 'production line' helps us to not fall into the trap of becoming too passionate about the idea before we have been able to assess it from as many different angles as possible.

ideas generation

What do we mean by 'assess'? We will get to that in Chapter 8, but for now let's go through the first seven steps of the Pophouse 21 Step Ideas Production Line (S.I.m.P.L.e.) These first seven steps will help you to generate thousands of ideas for yourself, your business and your future.

Step 1:
Thinking Big

There is absolutely nothing wrong with thinking big. In fact, if you don't think big and see what your grand vision could potentially look like, it will be much harder for you to keep working when the going gets tough (and it's going to every now and then!).

This means that you are starting at the end first. At Pophouse we call this *'back-engineering'* – and it works.

Start at the end first
At Pophouse we believe that starting at the end first stops us from sabotaging our ideas before they have even had the chance to breathe. Know your outcomes. See the biggest picture possible. Decide what you want your end result to be.

Let's assume your idea is the creation of a new fast-food chain. Do you want to revolutionise the fast food market? How many franchises do you want to have? How do you want the press to write about your business? Where do you want your idea to take you in five years' time – in ten years' time? How do you want to be remembered in the fast-food world? Which competitors will shiver on hearing your name?

If you can start at the end first, you can often see a clearer way of getting there. Often an idea will only become apparent once you have thought it all the way through to its end conclusion.

Some people call this visualising, others call it a positive affirmation. We call it 'back-engineering'. Call it anything you like. It all amounts to the same thing – thinking big!

If you can see the possibilities of your idea in terms of an end result, then you can go back to the beginning again and fill in the missing pieces. Back-engineering will force you to stick to your roadmap and will constantly remind you that there is a potential result to your idea.

Exercise

Draw a funnel (like below) on a blank piece of paper and write in a five-year time line. At the broadest end of the funnel write your end result. Keep your 'end result' drawing in a place where you can see it, such as the wall of your kitchen or bedroom or workspace.

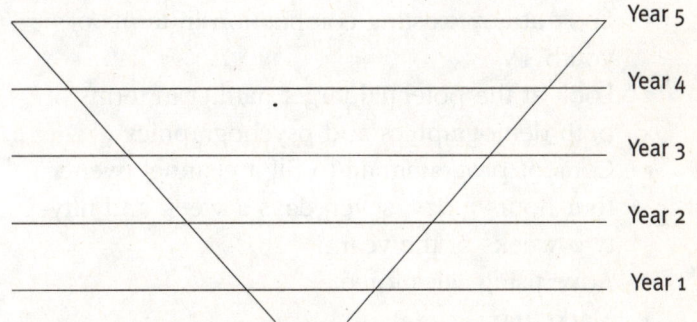

Year 5

Year 4

Year 3

Year 2

Year 1

Apply a magnifying glass to the idea

This is all about blowing up your idea so that you can see all its components. Think literally of how you can put a magnifying glass to your idea so that you can start to see

ideas generation

all of the detail. You need to see the fine print. As the old saying goes, the devil's in the detail!

What is really involved in getting your idea off the ground?

How complex will it be to make your idea a reality?

Will you need a partnership to make it happen?

Can you cover all the detail on your own?

Let's start big and presume that our idea entails the launch of a new youth television channel on cable TV. The idea is to launch the most exciting TV channel intended to attract a core demographic audience aged between sixteen and twenty-five.

Now let's put a magnifying glass to that idea by listing all the things (in no particular order) that we would need to study in detail in order to fully understand the breadth and depth of the idea...

- Obtain distribution through a cable TV network
- Complete a full SWOT analysis – strengths, weaknesses, opportunities, threats
- Look at any existing competition in terms of youth TV
- Look at the potential target market in terms of both demographics and psychographics
- Content/programming to fill a channel twenty-four hours a day, seven days a week and fifty-two weeks of the year
- Advertising sales force
- Marketing
- Business plan
- Finance
- Staff – on air and off air
- International distribution

- Licensing opportunities
- Legal counsel
- Television programming expertise
- Youth programming and marketing expertise
- Seed capital
- Marketing and sales collateral
- Alliances and joint ventures with youth content developers – music, movies, video, computer games, clothing

And that's just the beginning! One of the best ways to see your idea is to list everything that your idea will need to cover in order to become a reality.

Exercise

Take one of your ideas and make a list of all the things you need to consider – even if it is something you yourself would not do but would outsource. Do not leave anything off the list. We'll start it for you.

MAGNIFYING GLASS LIST

1 _____
2 _____
3 _____
4 _____
5 _____
6 _____
7 _____
8 _____
9 _____
10 _____

ideas generation

Forget logistics

The single biggest killer of ideas is the logistics trap. The trap goes something like this:

"It's too hard"
"I can't possibly pull this off"
"It will take too much money"
"I don't have the experience"
"I'll get laughed out of the room"
"There is no way this will work"
"I'd have to dedicate my life to this"
"It's just too big an idea"
"There are so many components that have to fit together – it's too hard to forge alliances"
"Somebody else with lots more contacts and money will have the same idea and get there first"
"It's too new and I'm not sure there's a market for it"
"It's a pipe dream"
"I can't read numbers"
"I'm not an accountant"
"I'm out of my depth"
"How will this ever come together?"
"It's too complicated for me to break it down"

Now let's look at this list again and show you how to avoid this trap...

"It's too hard"	"Break down the process step by step"
"I can't possibly pull this off"	"I'll work to my strengths and out-source the stuff I don't know"
"It will take too much money"	"What does phase one cost?"
"I don't have the experience"	"I'll learn as I go and read everything I can get my hands on"
"There is no way this will work"	"What's the single biggest reason why this will work?"
"I'll get laughed out of the room"	"No one will laugh if I do my homework"
"I'd have to dedicate my life to this"	"If I love and believe in this idea then I can't but help enjoy my life"
"It's just too big an idea"	"A big idea can be broken down into smaller steps"
"There are so many components that have to fit together – it's too hard to forge alliances"	"Twenty-first-century business is all about alliances – think *Titanic*!"
"Somebody else with lots more contacts and money will have the same idea and get there first"	"All the great pioneers started with only one idea"
"It's too new and I'm not sure there's a market for it"	"I'll run the numbers and do the maths first"
"It's a pipe dream"	"All great ideas start as dreams"
"I can't read numbers"	"I have an accountant friend who can"
"I'm not an accountant"	"I can give away a small piece of equity for free accounting"
"I'm out of my depth"	"It will force me to keep moving forward"
"How will this ever come together?"	"One step at a time"
"It's too complicated for me to break it down"	"If I can't explain it clearly, I don't have a good idea"

ideas generation

Change the world

Don't be afraid to think of your idea as the potential invention of a new paradigm or a revolution in an industry.

Let's assume you have an idea that could revolutionise the computer industry – something like a mobile computer screen that rolls up into a tiny ball and could be attached to any computer, allowing access to files without the need of a server. An idea like this could threaten existing businesses and create an entirely new industry. A revolution would occur. Large multinationals could tumble and your technology could change the computer industry forever.

Exercise:

Draw a *paradigm map* like the one below:

THE INDUSTRY	MY IDEA
THE STATUS QUO	IS/HOW IS MY IDEA REVOLUTIONARY?

Step 2:

Criteria Matrix

A criteria matrix can help you build your ideas. What is a criteria matrix? A criteria matrix is a grid that will help you to improve and assess your ideas as you build them.

In the criteria matrix we use, we need to answer seven key questions with conviction, passion – and most importantly, with yes/no simplicity. Often we find that if it is hard for us to answer our seven key questions, we must find a better way of *articulating* the idea or we must *strengthen* and *clarify* the idea.

CRITERIA MATRIX

1. Is the idea simple to explain?
2. Is the idea simple to understand?
3. Is it the type of idea that makes people say "I wish I'd thought of that"?
4. Is the timing right?
5. Have individuals or companies with expertise offered to work on the idea in exchange for equity?
6. Has the market come to you?
7. Do you see trends in the marketplace that could help your idea come to life?

The criteria matrix should not be used as a way to stymie good thinking or assess an idea before it has ripened. On the contrary, it is a tool that can be used to clarify thinking and remind you, the ideas generator, of the potential gold you have in your possession.

Nor should the criteria matrix be used to throw out ideas or standardise the more unorthodox ones. Its intention is to help you see your idea for what it really is. Simple, strong, smart ideas are worth the investment of time and money.

ideas generation

The criteria matrix can also be used to help you look at your folder of ideas and prioritise them. Often when the criteria matrix is applied you can discover the ideas you are most attached to, have the most belief in, will work day and night to achieve, are proud to present and those that make the most common sense.

The one important factor that all the planning research and business modelling in the world cannot give you is faith in your idea. The criteria matrix will unlock your real internal instincts about your idea and help you draw on your self-reliance and self-confidence when detractors attempt to talk you out of your idea or, more importantly, try to steal your idea or acquire a larger piece of equity than they deserve.

The matrix will allow you to return to the truth of your idea when you lose sight of what you are trying to achieve. Believe us – it will happen from time to time!

Substituting Your Own Criteria Matrix

Just because we've chosen the seven criteria that work best for us doesn't mean that you can't change the criteria.

Recently, we generated an idea for a large international corporation and in order to 'see' the idea, we decided to change the matrix. The idea was to take the corporation's advertising campaign idea and turn it into an animated TV show. The thinking was to create a new revenue stream for the company by taking a property that was only intended to create brand presence for that company and turn it into TV programming.

There were a number of issues that we needed to look at – such as whether there would be any negative effect on the corporation's brand and how this branding extension would add to the corporation's bottom line.

In order to assess the effects of this idea, we redrew the criteria matrix as follows and allowed for the inclusion of yes/no questions as well as open-ended answers:

CRITERIA MATRIX

1. Does the existing creative advertising device say the right things about the corporation?
2. Does this creative device have a long-term shelf life?
3. What is the true value of the creative device in terms of brand image for the corporation?
4. How do we intend to make the brand more appealing by turning the creative property into TV programming?
5. Is the programming content good enough to stand alone as true content without the marketing support of the corporation?
6. How will the market share grow if the programming is created?
7. How will the programming affect the core business of the corporation?

Remember, the true reason behind the criteria matrix is to flush out the real issues behind the idea. Although it can and often will help you assess the quality of your idea and thus improve it, its ultimate reason for being is to tease out the real issues and hidden challenges you might have with the idea. Good luck matrixing!

ideas generation

Step 3:
Hunting and Gathering

Thousands of years ago in agrarian society, hunters and gatherers were the first strategists. They did their homework and took their time making sure they had all the things they needed to survive through the harshest of winters. They planned, became informed, experimented, learned, practised, manipulated, searched, travelled and trapped their information in order to become more knowledgeable about the world they found themselves living in.

Yes, it's true they did it for reasons of survival – but through this process, they became *educated*.

As an ideas generator, you must become absolutely committed to the pursuit of information gathering. You must make it your personal quest to build up the most comprehensive library of information that can possibly help you with your idea. A great man once said "A worker is only as good as his tools." It is also true that an ideas generator is only as good as his or her information-gathering skills.

You may think you've come up with the most fantastic idea in the whole world, or in the history of mankind. You won't feel quite so excited once you find out that there were 100 people before you who had exactly the same idea and it failed. Your idea could potentially be the 101st idea in the same vein of thinking, but the only one that works. There could be a tiny, tiny thing that makes your idea the winning idea, but you won't know any of this unless you know the history of the 100 ideas that failed before you.

The 100 failures before you should never discourage you – don't feel that by avoiding the research you will avoid self-doubt. Reading about the 100 failures before you should make you feel stronger and braver and more confident because you can also see why the other 100 ideas failed.

Often we hear people say that they don't read anything, that they never hunt and gather because they don't want to get discouraged when they are in the ideas generation process.

Nonsense! Fearing information is like fearing oxygen. Be open to new information – to anything that could be important to your idea.

We can hear some of you ask, *"But what about information overload?"*

Our answer to that is that there is no such thing. The human mind has an amazing way of blocking out the useless stuff. Just keep pouring information into your body and your mind will tell you when it is full – when you have enough to feel confident about your idea and feel confident that you have done your homework.

The big question is where to find the good information.

Ah, now you're asking the right question! This is one of our specialities!

You have to think about it like this. There are literally millions of people who are generating ideas. And the good ideas generators are hunters and gatherers. They are gathering their information just as you are. They are reading the newspapers every day. They are reading magazines, surfing the Internet, talking to people, attending conferences, going to movies, listening to music, reading books.

ideas generation

The real question is, how do you separate yourself from the pack, how do you give yourself the advantage? By gathering the most unusual information, by going outside the predictable sources of information – by being creative even in the way you gather the information.

When George Lucas came up with the idea of the *Star Wars* trilogy, he took the unusual step of speaking with sociologists and anthropologists from major universities in order to study the notions of good versus evil. Although many millions have interpreted his movies as great action flicks delivering spectacular special effects, the deeper analysis of his movies are about the motivations of people and of humanity in general. Why are people evil – what made Darth Vader such an evil character, why do evil forces continually attempt to control society and why should forces of good fight back?

Lucas' hunting and gathering went way beyond discovering the latest technology to create amazing special effects.

Example

Let's assume we have an idea for a new type of dog shampoo. Our idea is to create a shampoo for dogs that keeps their hair clean for a longer period of time. Where would we begin to gather information about this topic?

First we would start by purchasing all of the existing products on the market to see what the competition is currently doing. We can then discover all the ingredients that go into a dog shampoo. We'd probably find that it isn't too dissimilar to human shampoo.

We'd then purchase all the publications on dogs and dog grooming. We'd also visit a dog grooming salon to see if any of the products they use are different to the products currently selling on the market.

We'd then talk to experts in the field – dog groomers, dog shampoo manufacturers, scientists.

We'd surf the Internet to see what information exists on the market – areas like dog products, shampoos, any research and development in the area.

This is all standard information that any good hunter and gatherer can find.

Then we need to start searching for the more unique information. Because we haven't extended our information search beyond the obvious we need to think more about the idea. We might ask ourselves this: What would be the true purpose of this product and what would be its key benefit and why would a dog owner think this is a great product?

Then we might think about other industries that face similar problems. So we get our first brainwave – Scotchguard! We then start to research Scotchguard and how it protects fabrics from dirt and spots. Now we're getting somewhere!

Our information search suddenly takes a new twist. We ask ourselves whether it is possible to create a new type of dog shampoo that is almost like Scotchguard – so that if Rover has a bath and gets really dirty on his walk, can he be hosed down and restored to his formerly clean self?

Now we need to seek out information on safe chemicals and find out how this process could work on a dog. We would need to check whether it is scientifically possible, whether it is humane, whether the RSPCA would object.

We would need to look at other factors like the demographic trends.

ideas generation

- How many dogs are there in the country?
- How much money does the average dog owner spend on grooming products for their dog?
- Is keeping the family dog clean a problem for dog owners?
- How often does the average dog get a bath?
- Who does the bathing – the kids or mum and dad?
- How many dog-grooming salons are there in the country?

Now we would need to go to places where this information is available. Places like the Bureau of Statistics, the RSPCA and professional canine associations.

See how we've extended our information gathering beyond the boundaries of our idea?

Exercise
Make a list of all the sources of information you have at your fingertips. Then make a second list of things you think might stretch you beyond your circle of thinking. Use our example to help you flesh out your information list.

Step 4:
Deliberately Break the Rules

This is one of our favourites! Deliberately breaking the rules is all about thinking all the thoughts you're not supposed to.

More importantly, it's about being open to the possibilities of your idea when the world and everyone in it is saying it can't be done. You have to forget about what's possible, you have to forget about societal norms, you have to forget about the obvious. Basically, you have to forget about the rules.

When the ancient Greeks won the battle of Marathon against the Persians, they did it by ignoring the rules of conventional warfare. The general leading the Greek army had a significantly smaller army than the Persians. The great challenge was to find a place to have the battle that would be significantly advantageous to the Greeks. If the battle were to be fought on an open field, the huge Persian army, whose forces were numbered in the thousands, would surely slaughter all the Greeks.

The general was told that it would be impossible to win the battle and that he should surrender rather than face inevitable defeat. Forced to come up with a new strategy, he deliberately broke the rules of warfare that said a smaller army could never win against a larger and better equipped one.

What he did was this. He led the Persians into a narrow passageway and tricked them into thinking that this would be their easiest victory in the history of warfare. He weakened his centre, leaving only a limited number

ideas generation

of troops to meet the enemy whilst keeping his flanks strong. The Persians entered the trap arrogantly and as they overran the centre of the Greek army, the flanks quickly moved to encircle the entire Persian army. The Greeks won the battle in what has become one of the most heroic victories in the history of warfare.

This is a great lesson for us all. Why can't it be done? Who says? The critics. The cynics. The cowards.

Let's look at an example closer to home. Everybody remembers the near tragedy on Apollo 13. The astronauts had to find enough power in the shuttle to get back to earth. The ground team were able to find a way of getting the maximum voltage out of a 12-volt battery and the rest is history.

Let's assume you have an idea that sounds impossible – an idea to prevent every traffic jam in every modern city of the world. The critics would immediately say: *"It's impossible, there's no way you can plan the traffic in advance. Unexpected things happen and all traffic volume is dependent on so many other factors."*

Now it's your turn to deliberately break the rules. Broken rule number 1 – you can plan the traffic flow at every moment of the day. The idea might be to create a satellite navigational system that can 'radar' all of the traffic within a 200-kilometre radius. The system then tells the driver how much traffic is in the area and how many people using the same technology have elected to take that route. Updates are in real time and every driver knows the traffic situation in their area and along their journey.

All governments then legislate to have all car manufacturers place this navigational system in every new automobile as a compulsory unit and at registration time, place the technology in old cars as well.

The DBR Game

The Deliberately Breaking the Rules game is a way of training your mind to say yes when your nature is to say no.

The rules of the game are as follows:

- Think of something you know that has an absolute truth attached – for example, that a soufflé always takes forty-five minutes to bake.
- Break down the reasons why you believe this to be the case.
- Go through the process of making a soufflé.
- See if there is any way to shorten the length of time it takes to make a soufflé.
- Force yourself to see the possibilities.

By the way, somebody recently worked out that a soufflé can be made in twenty minutes and has revolutionised the restaurant industry.

Let's go through the process again:

- Think of an absolute truth.
- Examine the reasons why you think it is an absolute truth.
- Go through the process of how that absolute truth comes into being.
- See if that process can be changed.
- Force yourself to see the possibilities.

This step is a great way for you to generate thousands of ideas for yourself, your business and your future. It can also double your success rate. It will help you to avoid linear thought by making unexpected connections. Above all it will help you create a context for divergent thinking. Deliberately breaking the rules is all about going where no man (or woman) has gone before. Where others fear to generate ideas, you must stretch yourself to go!

Step 5:
Timing is Everything

An incredibly fertile way of generating thousands of ideas is to look at the cycles of time.

Think of the fashion industry. Everything is cyclical. Just take a look at today's fashion trends and see how some of yesterday's fashions are today's hot new look.

Ever heard the saying 'an idea whose time has come'? Sometimes you might have the best idea in the world but the timing isn't quite right.

Remember Beta videocassette recorders? If you said 'yes', you are in the minority. Beta was a revolution in the television and entertainment industry. This amazing technology called a VCR could record TV shows while its owner was away on holiday. It was able to let the viewer watch one channel while recording another. It was an absolutely sensational idea.

Except for one thing. The timing. The market was a little hesitant about buying into this technology and the idea of a VCR seemingly came a little early.

Roughly a year later an alternative operating system was invented called VHS. VHS videocassette recorders performed exactly the same technology as the Beta VCR and were an instant hit in the market place. Analysts today are still asking themselves why.

It's a pretty simple reason actually. The Beta VCR had laid the groundwork for the VHS VCR. Beta as a pioneer had spent one year educating the market, getting the price point right, convincing retailers to sell the machine, creating advertising to promote the availability of the technology and all the other one million things that go into establishing a new product line within a brand-new industry. It is no surprise that Beta failed whilst VHS came in on the back on Beta's excellent groundwork

The truth is that the Beta system offered superior technology. But because the timing was wrong it never made any difference. Being twelve months too early is a cautionary tale for all ideas generators today. An idea that you present in 2000 may not seem compelling today but in five years it could be the biggest idea going.

That's why it is important for you to keep all of your ideas on file. Never throw away what you think is a bad idea. It might not be intrinsically bad – just an idea that does not suit today's environment.

So how do you understand the issue of timing?

The best way to do this is to understand and identify Signs of the Times.

How does this work?

Identifying Signs of the Times is a process of writing down all the connected signs that are dropped in your lap from the universe.

Example: You have an idea to start a courier company specialising in the delivery of gourmet dinners to late-working city executives. The reason why your courier company is different is that it works exclusively with the top seven restaurants in the city. These couriers are

ideas generation

experts at delivering the food so that it is hot, still beautifully arranged and presented with all the necessary condiments and cutlery.

Now let's identify the Signs of the Times that have led you to this idea.

- City executives working 55 hours per week on average.
- 3 in 10 workers regularly work past 7pm three evenings a week.
- Companies willing to feed their top people good food without a moment's hesitation in order to keep them working longer hours productively and continually.
- Another reason to stay late and finish today what used to be able to be put off until tomorrow.
- No courier companies work past 7pm except under special circumstances.
- Top restaurants realise that to be profitable they need to continue creating new revenue streams.
- Difficult to get good quality take-away food in the cities of Australia.
- Demand for top-quality food on the increase.
- Food connoisseurs growing by the hundreds every day in Australia.
- New definition of take-out ready to hit society.

Now look at your Sign of the Times list and see if there is another idea you would like to explore. Let us give you an example we recently experienced.

We were generating ideas in an attempt to come up with a new idea for a children's toy. We had decided to look at something electronic and settled on an idea to create a type of mini palm-pilot for kids where they could record their friends' names and addresses electronically. It seemed a good idea suited to the knowledge and ease kids have about technology.

We then wrote our Sign of the Times list. Number four on that list was the feeling that children today have a much more sophisticated attitude when it comes to their friendships. They call their friends after school (even if they are in the second grade), and they seem to be invited to as many organised functions as do grown-up socialites.

Then it struck us. We realised that children love to show their friends how much they care about them. Being someone's best friend is what many if not all children seek. What about a line of friendship bracelets and other trinkets designed to show a friend how much he or she is valued? Our idea was in fact the opposite of high-tech. It was simple, strong, appealing and very marketable!

Exercise

Apply one of your ideas to the Signs of the Times. Think of at least five signs to go on your list. It doesn't matter how obscure or disconnected you think they might be. If you believe it is a sign, put it down. It is amazing how often these signs themselves also lead you to creating new ideas. Don't be surprised if you start with one idea and end up exploring another. Don't worry about being too exacting on yourself when it comes to your list. Just get it down on paper. Even if you feel that you don't have enough evidence to support your theory, don't worry – just write it down.

ideas generation

Step 6:
Creating the Future

Creating the future is all about casting your mind three, five, even ten years ahead and imagining how the world might change and what types of things you might need in the future.

Creating the future is about letting your imagination run wild. Because the future doesn't exist, there are no boundaries and nobody can tell you that something is impossible.

The beauty of this step is that you can get to the future before anybody else gets there.

The first thing we want you to do is to complete the following exercise:

Exercise
Take a large blank piece of paper and copy the following grid:

	2002	2005	2007	2010
LEISURE				
ENTERTAINMENT				
WORK				
HOME				

In each of the boxes write down the types of things you think will change in the future. We'll give you our version of the leisure grid.

	2002	2005	2007	2010
LEISURE	Less time for organised holidays. TV shows and game shows on leisure Pretend leisure – clothing lines that you can wear on weekends that make you feel like you've gone on holiday Nature trips rather the five-star experiences.	Workers demanding more leisure time. Leisure arcades. Leisure cities, where work is forbidden.	Historical holidays – ancient ruins Everything old is new again. Travel to old, historic places. Going back in time.	Virtual holidays Travelling to the future. Virtual space travel

Once you've finished filling out the grid, look at all of the 'predictions' you have come up with.

Look at each one in isolation and write down as many ideas on paper as you have for each of the predictions. Let's take one of our predictions from 2002.

ideas generation

Prediction: Virtual holidays

Ideas list
- Come up with ideas for software/games that take you on a virtual holiday.
- Come up with an idea of books and/or places that people would most like to go to on their virtual holiday.
- Generate ideas for TV shows and virtual holidays, merchandise that can be sold to people as an escape and a substitute for a real holiday.

The point of creating the future is that you are not bound by the real – only by the imaginary. As we all know, imagination has no limits.

It's all about taking an excursion from the mundane and the predictable. By travelling into the future, we can take a leave of absence from the boundaries of our own minds and live in the world that does not yet exist.

Taking a mental holiday is often the best way to kick-start your creative juices. The creative boundaries are immediately removed and you can dream up ideas that are not in any way, shape or form connected to reality.

Another great advantage of creating the future is that you can act as though the idea you are working on has worked and has become a successful idea in society.

Let's go back to our idea of the virtual holiday and assume that people have been taking virtual holidays for years.

Then we start to think about some of the other things that people on virtual holidays might desire. If they have already been taking virtual holidays, then what about virtual diets, virtual children, virtual relationships, virtual marriage, virtual massage?...

As long as you are able to think in a future context you will find yourself able to create new ideas. It's amazing how freeing the future can be for your mind. Remember to take an excursion into the future on a regular basis!

Step 7:
Using Force Fields

Force Fields are the best way of changing the status quo. Using Force Fields is a simple way of shaking things up and confronting a stagnant situation. It is an excellent tool for analysing an existing situation and nudging it into the direction you want it to go.

Think of Force Fields like a very large magnet applied to your idea. The magnet is supposed to pull your idea into the direction you want it to travel.

Here's how to use it:

1. **Use a large sheet of paper and draw a diagram like this:**

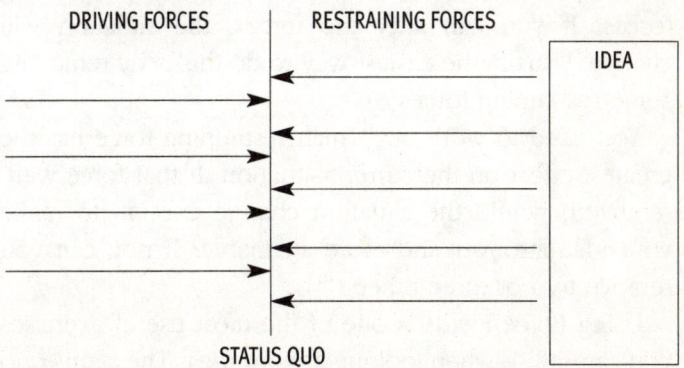

```
DRIVING FORCES    |    RESTRAINING FORCES
                  |                        ┌──────┐
                  |                        │ IDEA │
         ────────>│<────────────           │      │
                  |                        │      │
         ────────>│<────────────           │      │
                  |                        │      │
         ────────>│<────────────           │      │
                  |                        │      │
         ────────>│<────────────           │      │
                  |                        │      │
         ────────>│<────────────           │      │
                  |                        └──────┘
              STATUS QUO
```

ideas generation

- After you've written up this diagram, brainstorm all the forces in the current situation that are driving you toward your desired result.
- Then brainstorm all the restraining forces in the current situation that are keeping the changes you want from happening.

We'll start the grid for you...

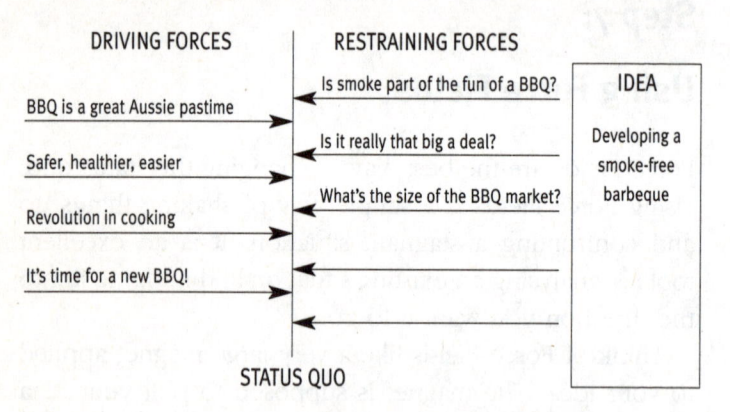

DRIVING FORCES	RESTRAINING FORCES	IDEA
BBQ is a great Aussie pastime	Is smoke part of the fun of a BBQ?	Developing a smoke-free barbeque
Safer, healthier, easier	Is it really that big a deal?	
Revolution in cooking	What's the size of the BBQ market?	
It's time for a new BBQ!		

STATUS QUO

Once the chart is completed, sit back and analyse it for the easiest way to change the status quo.

The present situation is held in place by opposing forces. If you can alter the forces, the situation will change. Usually the easiest way to do this is by removing some restraining forces.

You need to work out which restraining force has the greatest effect on the current situation. If that force were removed, would the situation change enough to make your idea stronger and more attainable? If not, can you remove two or three others?

Using Force Fields is one of the most useful exercises you can utilise when looking at your idea. The status quo is there to be broken and manipulated. Force Fields is one of the best ways to push your idea further along the development chain and construct new ways to shape and improve the idea.

Let us give you another example.

We came up with an idea for a new laundry detergent. This laundry detergent was going to carry the Pophouse brand name and was to be marketed to the youth market – first-time home buyers, first-time renters, university students sharing houses.

We filled in our Force Fields grid and this is what it looked like…

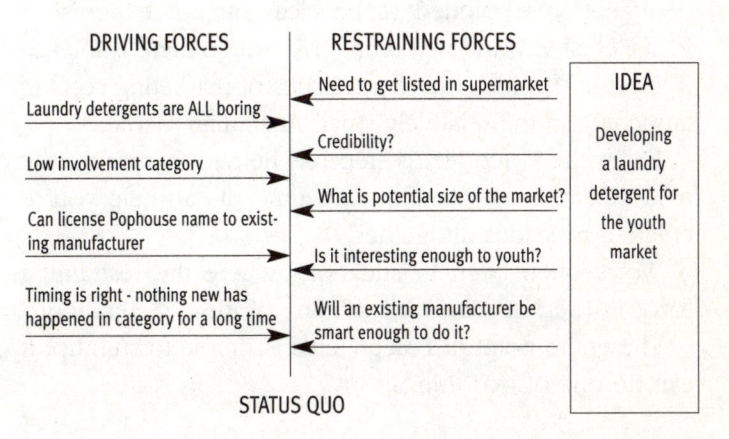

DRIVING FORCES	RESTRAINING FORCES	IDEA
Laundry detergents are ALL boring	Need to get listed in supermarket	Developing a laundry detergent for the youth market
Low involvement category	Credibility?	
Can license Pophouse name to existing manufacturer	What is potential size of the market?	
	Is it interesting enough to youth?	
Timing is right - nothing new has happened in category for a long time	Will an existing manufacturer be smart enough to do it?	

STATUS QUO

We needed to take away some of the very large restraining forces – particularly the one concerning distribution. We needed to be able to neutralise this restraining force by securing distribution through our joint venture or licensee partner, the manufacturer.

We also needed to work out if the potential market size could be larger than just the youth demographic – so we needed to make sure that we were marketing to a group of people who feel young and not only to those who happen to be under the age of thirty.

By spending some time working on the removal of the restraining forces we were able to see our idea more clearly and improve its potential success rate.

We felt very strongly that the idea would work, as the laundry detergent category was extremely staid and uninteresting. Imagine if we could market a fun detergent with an amazing Andy Warhol style box design and turn the packaging into a form of Pop-Art. Pophouse laundry detergent would be the perfect name!

As we are not a detergent manufacturing company and would not know the first thing about manufacturing detergents, we needed to be clear on our expertise – ideas, creativity and marketing. (Although there is intense interest in this idea, there are issues of marketing costs in launching in the relatively small Australian market.)

Using the Force Fields step has helped us to generate a stronger, better idea and sometimes it can help you to create a new idea altogether.

We've often been in situations where the restraining force in itself becomes a goldmine of ideas generation!

The entire point of Force Fields is simple to sum up. It can do one of two things:

- It can improve the quality of the existing idea.
- It can open up a new path of ideas generation where the restraining and driving forces can each present you with new ideas of their own. Think of it like a tree that spawns its own seedlings. You may have started out with only one idea but end up with scores of ideas.

After all, remember what we said in our opening chapter. In order to have one good idea you need to create hundreds. Do not be precious about your ideas – just keep creating them. Being prolific with your ideas generation is the key!

Abundance of ideas generation is the goal. Force Fields is one excellent way for you to multiply the number of ideas you can generate – because if you go back to our laundry detergent example and look at just one of the restraining forces (will an existing manufacturer be smart enough to do it?), we were able to come up with a whole new list of ideas based on that restraining force:

- Offer a creative service to the industry.
- Develop a licensing company that licenses the Pophouse name.
- Commission an art exhibition that treats detergent boxes like art.
- Avoid manufacturers and make it ourselves in limited quantities and get distribution in specialty stores and service stations.

The key to using Force Fields is to use them when you're getting tired – when you need a fresh perspective to help you generate ideas.

Think of it as just another tool in your ideas generator toolkit – just another of the steps to ideas generation.

7

The 21 Step Ideas Production Line: S.I.m.P.L.e. Steps 8 to 14

How to spot the great ideas from the not-so-great. Grading and storing ideas. Simmering ideas slowly, cooking them gently. Incubating your ideas. Techniques for maintaining perspective. Investigating and editing ideas.

Steps 8 to 14 in the ideas generation process are all about spotting the winners from the stinkers. Well, no idea really stinks – its success depends on its timing and manipulation. There still might be something of value in it, so remember – never throw any of your ideas away! Store them for a later date. You never can tell when they might come in handy.

Grading your ideas and storing the others for a later date is an artform within itself. This next chapter should give you some pointers on how to do this effectively and succinctly. Simmering ideas is an excellent habit to form. Like a good sauce, simmering is often the key. Over time,

ideas generation

cooking your ideas slowly and gently can bring out their flavour.

Every idea needs some time to incubate before it hatches. The following chapter will give you some techniques for maintaining perspective and for investigating, editing and selecting the ideas that have a better chance of success.

Step 8:

Brutal Truth (BT)

Although this step may sound very, very scary – it's supposed to! A little bit of fear is good for every idea that thinks its time has come.

Brutal truth is all about uncovering the issues, challenges, problems and liabilities of your idea. It is the process of being completely honest with yourself about it. Don't get defensive or despondent; Brutal Truth (BT) is not intended to shut your creative thinking down or to insult your idea, but rather to help you improve on some of its weaknesses. It also reminds us all that unless we are able to handle criticism we should find a more relaxing profession! Self-criticism is healthy, even critical to the idea generation process.

All we ideas generators need to be toughened up and remember the cardinal rule: Ideas are a dime a dozen. Anyone can have them. It is the ones that become reality that mean something.

When Garry Marshall was making *Pretty Woman*, the top-grossing movie starring Julia Roberts, he knew the script in its original form had some room for improvement. He also knew that he had something good in his hands but was truthful enough with himself to change the script considerably, thereby taking the script and changing it from a drama to a comedy.

Do not be afraid to challenge your idea and change it considerably – now is the time to go through this process.

There are two processes you can run your idea through, depending whether you want to share it with others or keep it to yourself. We've spoken before in this book (and will speak again) about protecting your ideas, and the dangers you can face in sharing them.

Some say it's a matter of trust. We say: Trust no-one when it comes to the sharing of your ideas. Best friends can turn into your worst enemies and your idea could turn up on a supermarket shelf. Remember – it is extremely difficult to protect ideas. Copyright, patents and trademarks can only do some of the job. A competitor can take your idea, change a few things and say they had a similar idea as well. Two people in a world of more than one billion can have a similar idea at almost the same time.

Others feel they can trust a group of people who can help them and become excellent sounding boards. This is your personal decision, but we have learned the hard way. Be careful. We leave it in your hands.

BT PROCESS ONE:
KEEPING YOUR IDEAS CONFIDENTIAL

Write your idea in the centre of a piece of paper and draw two columns – one on either side of the paper. In each of the columns place the words 'weaknesses' and

ideas generation

'threats' in each column. Your job is to fill the two columns up completely. Don't be shy – be brutal! We'll demonstrate with our dog shampoo idea from Chapter 7.

> **DOG SHAMPOO**
> Works like Scotchguard by washing hair and protecting dog from dirt for a period of up to four weeks.

WEAKNESSES (W)	THREATS (T)
No demand from market place	Probably already in R&D
Dogs are not humans	Scotchguard could sue
Size of market too small	Idea could be stolen by industry
Do dog owners really care about dirt?	No RSPCA approval – no product
Inhumane	Time to market
No knowledge of shampoo technology	
Expensive R&D	
Can't be used on cats and other pets/animals	
Would have to sell idea	

The W/T Chart will allow you to place as much weight of doubt on your idea as possible. You don't need to keep up with good reasons as to why the idea will work – we'll do that in another step. The goal here is to sabotage and suffocate the idea. The truth is that an excellent idea is hard to kill. It has a strange way of popping its head up all the time.

Remember that this is what the market place will try to do to your idea every time. When it comes time to present your idea to the decision makers, they will spend

7 The 21 Step Ideas Production Line: Steps 8 to 14

their time coming up with all the reasons why the idea won't work. You need to have done this process first – so that if you decide to continue developing the idea you have all the rebuttals to their gloomy forecasts about your idea.

You need to have thought about what the downsides are before the 'selection committee' go through the process – and in a way more brutal than you could ever do to the idea yourself! This process will achieve three things. It will:

- Flush out a half-baked imposter idea
- Help you improve the weaknesses of the idea
- Make you much stronger and more confident if you eventually present the idea

BT PROCESS TWO: ASKING THE EXPERTS

This Brutal Truth process is about sharing your ideas with others and asking for their feedback – though remember our warning about sharing ideas.

This process is about finding some 'experts' who can assess your idea. These experts need to possess qualities and skills that you do not possess – technical know-how, political savvy, deeper background information. Your sources might include other people in your organisation, professors from local universities, researchers, writers, leaders in the business community.

The point of this exercise is to recruit a panel of experts or a single expert related directly to the idea or the needs that you must fulfil.

For example, if we go back to our dog shampoo idea, we need to speak with chemists who manufacture dog shampoo, and experts in cleaning things dirt-free. We

ideas generation

might also speak to a dog expert or somebody at the RSPCA or related canine associations. We've started the list to show how it might be different from BT process one.

DOG SHAMPOO
Works like Scotchguard by washing hair and protecting dog from dirt for a period of up to four weeks.

WEAKNESSES	THREATS
Too expensive to produce	Three companies already have a patent out
Size of dog market declining	RSPCA has already knocked back the idea
Growth in dog grooming salons	

Brutal Truth is all about facing the realities of your idea and staring them square in the face. It will also uncover some of the things that have been bothering you and some of the things you have been avoiding.

Best of all, it will give you your first real insight into how prepared you need to be once you have decided to present your idea to the world!

Step 9:

Lowest Hanging Fruit

Lowest Hanging Fruit is the term we use to describe the ideas that are the:

7 The 21 Step Ideas Production Line: Steps 8 to 14

- easiest to achieve
- easiest to explain
- simplest to defend
- strongest
- most opportunistic.

Like the lowest hanging fruit, they should be easy to pick off the ideas tree, because they seem the most logical and carry the greatest reserve of common sense.

Often the ideas that are easiest to sell attract the response: *"That's so simple, I could have thought of that..."*

Again this step is about helping you identify the winners and hone the ideas that are worth continually working on and improving.

The Lowest Hanging Fruit Grid looks something like this:

SCORE/10

IDEA		
PROCESS TO ACHIEVE		
WAY TO EXPLAIN		
HOW TO DEFEND		
STRENGTHS		
OPPORTUNITIES		
SLIPSTREAM		
LUCK		
CONTACTS		
EVIDENCE/TRENDS		

The explanations for each of the steps in the grid are as follows:

ideas generation

Process to Achieve
How many obstacles are there to overcome in bringing this idea into reality? Is the process clear and direct? Is it relatively linear? How many hurdles need to be cleared? Will the process take a great deal of time?

Way to Explain
How simple is this idea to explain? Will the audience understand and see it immediately? Is it a convoluted explanation? Is there an immediately exciting presentation that goes with the idea?

How to Defend
How easy is the idea to defend? Are any tricky questions easy to address? Is there evidence that makes this idea very defensible?

Strengths
What are the strengths of this idea? Are there many? Can this idea stand on its own feet without being knocked down immediately by the critics?

Opportunities
Are there any opportunity by-products from this idea? Could an industry be revolutionised? Could other ideas fall out the back of this idea?

Slipstream
Could this idea ride on the back of one already in the market? Is there a way to 'slipstream' another good idea or occurrence in the market place? Is there some media attention the idea could capitalise on?

Luck
Does the idea feel lucky? Has the idea generation process to date seem blessed somehow or easier than most ideas that you have worked on?

Contacts
Does the idea allow you to capitalise on existing contacts that you have in your business or industry or line of work? Are there people who could easily become champions of the idea?

Evidence/trends
Is there some existing sound evidence to suggest that the idea will work? Are there trends in the market place that can help to explain the idea's potential success?

		SCORE/10
IDEA	CINEMA WITH RECLINING CHAIRS, BLANKETS AND TABLE SERVICE	9
PROCESS TO ACHIEVE	Everyone familiar with current cinema experience; simply an extension of current offerings in cinema	8
WAY TO EXPLAIN	Bring to life the experience by designing a presentation on storyboards	8
HOW TO DEFEND	Consumer focus groups and quantitative research showing that almost 70 per cent of Australians go to the cinema every year	10
STRENGTHS	Demand from market place, easy to put idea into practice	10
OPPORTUNITIES	Test-market idea with chain of cinemas	8
SLIPSTREAM	Some cinemas already providing nicer cinema experience – some already providing 'premiere' service	9
LUCK	Cinema attendance is the number one leisure and entertainment activity in Australia	10
CONTACTS	Know someone in the industry	8
EVIDENCE/TRENDS	Cinema attendance, consumers happy to pay for premium offering at double the ordinary price	10

ideas generation

Let's take one of our ideas and test out the Lowest Hanging Fruit Grid.

The purpose of the Lowest Hanging Fruit Grid is to assess the relative strength of your idea against others and to remind you of the advantages you have with one idea over another.

This grid also allows you to feel confident about an idea and reminds you that you have many weapons in your arsenal to explain and present your idea as a solid one that demands further investigation.

The key benefit of the grid is to separate your ideas with real possibilities from those that would take so much longer to massage into a decent and presentable shape.

It will also enable you to embrace the obvious ideas. As we have said before, obvious ideas can find themselves being pushed into the market at a very fast pace.

By using the Lowest Hanging Fruit Grid, you can prioritise your ideas and start to concentrate on the ideas that are solid and have a decent chance of success. Many a great inventor has had great success taking seemingly obvious ideas and finding investors to back them.

There is also a very positive experience to be had after applying the Lowest Hanging Fruit Grid to your idea. Let's face it – after the Brutal Truth experience, you will probably need some positive reinforcement!

Step 10:

Priority Matrix

It can be extremely difficult to mentally juggle all the factors needed to rank a list of more then five ideas in priority order without overlooking something important or missing out on looking more closely at a great idea. The Priority Matrix is a very helpful tool for prioritising as many ideas as you have. It works because it focuses you on one idea at a time.

The important thing to do is to come up with a list of eight criteria against which to judge the priority of an idea. Again, the purpose of these priorities is to list the ideas in order of importance, so you can judge which one to tackle first.

The sifting and ordering of ideas is an extremely important process because it forces you to focus on the ideas that have the best chance of succeeding.

The challenge with multiple ideas generation is that it is very easy to run ahead in a number of different directions without finding a sense of focus. Better to focus on two or three key ideas than to spend precious time simultaneously developing every one you have without really concentrating on a few.

What you must look for in your ideas is quality. The ideas you feel have the best chance of success are also those you will put your heart and soul into. This is an extremely important point. It is very difficult to concentrate on ideas development without believing in them. Passion and commitment keep you going into the wee hours of the morning.

Passion also keeps you going when you are tired, sick of the hard work it takes to get an idea off the ground, despondent, losing confidence, losing sight of the bigger picture, feeling alone and frankly going mad with imagination and possibilities rather than concrete results and fact.

Here's how to do it:

ideas generation

On a large sheet of paper create a grid with two identical lists of items you want to prioritise. One list will go horizontally down the left-hand side of the grid, the other will go vertically along the top. Place in the grid the criteria you would like to make your priority. Remember – you can put anything into the grid you like! Then you need to rate each idea against the priority matrix.

	originality	time to develop	potential $	number of buyers	size of market	passion for idea
Originality	X					
Time to develop						
Potential $			X			
Number of buyers						
Size of market						
Passion for idea						

Start with the first item on the vertical list and compare it to each item on the horizontal list.

Ask which is more important or desirable. For example, is it more important for your idea to be original or for it to have a large potential market size? If it is more important for your idea to be original, you can place an 'X' in the box, as we have. If it is more important that your idea have the potential large size of market, place the 'X' in the appropriate box.

Continue until you have compared all the criteria and filled in the grid.

Now count the number of times each item was selected. Record the total for each somewhere on the chart – along the right side, at the bottom or on another sheet. The item selected most often has the top priority.

7 The 21 Step Ideas Production Line: Steps 8 to 14

If an item wasn't selected at all, drop it from the list.

Recopy the list in priority order. If two or more items are tied, review the matrix:

- Look at where you compared two items to each other.
- The one you selected on the grid in the higher in priority.

This is just one of the ways you can prioritise your ideas and work out those you believe are strongest and most likely able to be developed. It will also help you to see the ideas you are really attached to and believe in.

The entire point of this exercise is to choose some ideas to concentrate on and put others into the filing cabinet.

Unless you do this process honestly and regularly, you are in danger of never being able to concentrate on one or two ideas. You will be doomed to ideas generation hell – never to proceed to the next level of ideas evaluation and assessment.

At this level you can also start to see the value of your idea crystallising and begin to focus on why you see this idea as a potential breakthrough. The important thing is for you to decide on the assessment criteria you need to select against which to measure your ideas. We have already given you some tips in previous steps – but ultimately it is up to you to decide how you will assess your ideas.

Once you start using this ideas generation production line, you will quickly get the hang of asking the right question and understanding how to assess the value and potential of your ideas. You will become an ideas evaluation professional!

ideas generation

This is perhaps one of the most important lessons you will learn. You will soon start to see your idea from the opposite side of the table and understand how easy it is for people to dismiss your ideas without even a second thought.

Like learning about fine wines, you will quickly start to learn what a good idea tastes like and smells like – and you will never be able to go back to ingesting half-baked ideas again.

Step 11:

Ideaweaving

There will come a point where you will have a difficult time deciding which option to go with because several options look promising or have good aspects, but no single idea is exciting. In these situations try weaving several ideas together. You may come up with a new option that is brilliant.

Ideaweaving is a great way of taking lots of 'scrap metal' and building a car. It's all about taking the little bits of ideas here and there and stitching them together into one very strong idea. The idea is that each of the smaller pieces in some strange way joins together to make for a much stronger whole.

It's true that often when you're struggling to identify a strong idea it's because the idea is missing the special ingredient that gives it that extra kick.

The Ideaweaving Exercise

Put each idea on a separate piece of paper. Write its name at the top. Do a plus or minus list under each idea, giving the top three to five advantages and disadvantages for each.

Post all of the idea charts along a wall.

Take a blank piece of paper and start developing a new idea that draws on the advantages and good features of several. Try to figure out how to minimise the disadvantages as you go. Put the disadvantages to one side and concentrate on improving the advantages.

You might find that you can pull out more than one new option this way.

Step 12:
Roleplaying – how would Einstein do this?

One of the best ways to clarify and sharpen your ideas is to see your idea from somebody else's perspective. Often it is a good idea to choose somebody you admire – or more specifically somebody's brain you admire and how they use it.

Role-playing stretches both your creative boundaries and gives you an analytical edge. Funny how we only ever see the strengths and weaknesses in an idea once we have viewed it from somebody else's point of view. Role-playing allows you to take a holiday from yourself and to tap into somebody else's mind and how that mind works.

ideas generation

This is a really fun way to see the angles of your idea, then start narrowing down and making choices.

Exercise
Stick a copy of your idea on a wall. Put a list of about ten famous names to serve as your consultants for this brainstorming session. Make sure the names represent widely different points of view. If you don't pick wildly different names you won't get a range of opinions about your idea.

The objective of this exercise is to focus and sharpen the quality of your idea.

Let's do an example together.

- Bart Simpson
- Albert Einstein
- Bill Clinton
- Marilyn Monroe
- Andrew Lloyd Webber
- John Wayne
- Madonna
- Joan of Arc
- Don King
- Jewel

The Idea
The idea is to develop a toothpaste tube with a lid that closes automatically. It doesn't matter if you forget to close the lid – it will close itself.

How would each of the people see this idea, how would they add to it, sharpen it, mould it, improve it, perfect it… Let's have a go!

7 The 21 Step Ideas Production Line: Steps 8 to 14

Bart Simpson
Things Bart would think...
- It should be marketed to men, because they are the ones who always forget to put the lid back on.
- The lid should make a noise when it's not closed.
- The toothpaste should glow in the dark.
- The tube should come with a Velcro holder

Albert Einstein
Things Albert Einstein would think...
- The design of the tube should be immediately patented and sold to every toothpaste manufacturing company.
- A premium should be charged for the tube design.
- The product should be called the thinking person's toothpaste.

Bill Clinton
Things Bill Clinton would think...
- The tube should be given out free to all the talk-show hosts of the world
- The tube should be marketed to disgruntled wives and girlfriends who can never get their partners to close the tube.
- The tube should be called Uncle Sam Toothpaste.

Marilyn Monroe
Things Marilyn Monroe would think...
- The sexiest people are always considerate about the toothpaste lid.
- The tube should come in all sizes for travel and at home.

ideas generation

- Product placement should be a priority in promoting the toothpaste.

Andrew Lloyd Webber
Things Andrew Lloyd Webber would think...
- A song should be produced about the virtues of this toothpaste.
- A free sample should be given with every travel ticket issued or hotel stay.
- A competition should be run to name the toothpaste brand.

John Wayne
Things John Wayne would think...
- A real man would always buy this toothpaste to be considerate.
- Why not call this the Western toothpaste?

You get the idea. Don't forget that the entire purpose of this step is to use somebody else's brain to creatively sharpen and improve your idea – it's also a lot of fun!

Don't be afraid to learn a little something about the person on your list. It may even give you a further insight into how to improve on your ideas and help you to choose the ideas with a lot of potential. Sometimes you'll find it is tough to separate the ideas creation from the ideas assessment.

That's OK. Don't stop yourself from generating a new idea. Just write it down on a piece of paper and go back to evaluating the idea. If you find that your mind has already begun to work on this new idea, go with it and don't fight it. Maybe you're just about to unlock the greatest idea of all time.

Step 13:
Editing

You may reach a point where your brain just can't work out whether your idea is good or not. Sometimes you can keep working on an idea, create lots of information to develop the idea without any clue as to whether it is quality thinking or not. Before you know it, you have streams of developed ideas and no clue as to whether you are on the right track. Think of it like this: a journalist can keep writing his or her story and submit it to the editor. It is the editor's job to clean it up, give it a sense of structure and narrative. Sometimes the best thing you can do is put your ideas away and leave them for a week or so. Don't even look at them, try not to think about them and definitely don't try an improve on them. Just let them sit quietly. After a week or so, take your idea out again and treat it with a sense of removal, in the same way an editor would treat a story. Treat it as though the idea does not belong to you, as though a friend has asked you to look at it in order to comment on the idea and improve on it. Try and pretend that you have seen the idea for the first time. Look at it without any baggage or personal commitment. Look at it with a sense of calm resolve. Yes – it's hard, but it is a wonderful way for you to remove yourself from your idea. This is an occasion on which you should remain passionless and objective. Try to remain relaxed throughout the entire process.

Editing is an extremely important skill to have. Take time perfecting the process. If it doesn't work the first time, put your ideas away and come back to it at a later date. This step is all about patience.

ideas generation

Step 14:
Incubation

It takes nine months for a baby to grow before it is ready to be born. Sometimes it can take years for an idea to gestate. Incubation is one of the most useful tools you have. (Just think about all the technology incubation labs throughout the world.)

Strange things happen to ideas when they are left on their own! They can take on a life of their own when left to their own devices. They seem to gather a taste and a vintage that no additional work and development can achieve. Other things seem to happen too.

Let us give you an example by using our idea of gourmet delivery dinners to busy executives working late nights in the office. Let's say it's your idea and you decide to let it incubate. You decide to let it sit under cover for a while.

Whilst it sits incubating, a couple of things happen…

- The number of people working increases dramatically.
- Key columnists write about how hard it is to get good takeaway food.
- Key gourmet restaurants start getting calls about late-night office delivery.
- Large organisations find themselves having to reimburse for takeaway pizza and Chinese food.
- A new restaurant opens up promising to give office workers good quality food into the small hours of the morning.

7 The 21 Step Ideas Production Line: Steps 8 to 14

You take your idea out of incubation and find that its time has come! And all you did was wait and let the idea cook a little further.

Another way to incubate ideas is to add a little something unusual into the mix and see what comes out the other end.

If we take our gourmet delivery idea one step further and add a twist so that the meal is delivered with top-quality wine and a waiter to serve the food then put it away, we can let it incubate for a while further and take it out later to see how it smells and tastes.

8

The 21 Step Ideas Production Line: S.I.m.P.L.e. Steps 15 to 21

Selling your ideas. Techniques for being heard. Defining a market for your ideas

Step 15:

Linear storytelling

Now you've learned how to generate thousands of ideas for your business or for yourself, they're really no good to you unless you can sell them to the market place.

The first thing you must learn is that good ideas are like stories well told. So all ideas generators need to learn to become excellent storytellers. In fact at Pophouse we believe storytelling will be the growth industry of the future. A good storyteller can make an idea come to life and secure enough seed capital to at least explore the idea more fully.

ideas generation

Linear storytelling is the skill of telling an 'ideas story' from beginning to end. One of the main problems of presenting an idea to an audience is lack of coherence. Linear storytelling is the art of telling only the important parts of the story without editorialising the parts that do not add to the development and process of idea development.

You don't want to give your audience too much information – only whatever is compelling and powerful. The information you give your audience will determine whether somebody else sees merit in your idea and ultimately whether there is the opportunity to get some investment and funding for it.

1. Set the context.
2. Give the background.
3. Tell your audience how the idea came into your head.
4. Divulge some personal information that allows your audience to get closer to the idea through you.
5. Break the idea into three parts.
6. Explain what effect it will have on the market and /or the world.
7. Give them some idea as to how you see this idea ending up.

Let's go through the process together by using our idea of gourmet office delivery.

1. **Set the context**

Something along the lines of...
Over 1.5 million office workers in Australia work a fifty-five-hour week or more. Of those, only 30 per cent have

dinner. The remaining 70 per cent don't bother eating anything because they don't like the options available and few restaurants cater to the CBD.

2. Give the background

A number of taxi drivers and courier drivers want to work after business hours – if there was work available. There are also a number of fine dining restaurants that would like to create a new revenue stream.

3. Tell your audience how the idea came into your head

You were working late one night in the office and you were hungry. You didn't want to order pizza and you felt like a great meal as you needed to keep focused all night. Your boss told you that they would be happy to reimburse any food expenses. So you got to thinking...

4. Divulge some personal information that allows your audience to get closer to the idea through you

You've always wanted to come up with an idea that was co-operative in nature – restaurants, couriers, taxis, waiters, bottle shops...you've always thought a great meal when you have to work back late is a great incentive to keep working.

5. Break the idea into three parts

Part One: A collective of the best restaurants in the city offering great takeaway meals to busy office workers.
Part Two: A collective of couriers and taxi drivers to deliver everything piping hot.
Part Three: A clever phone and marketing network to keep the whole thing humming along.

ideas generation

6. **Explain what effect it will have on the market and/or the world**

A potential market value of $20 million a year on sales and a much happier late-night office worker!

7. **Give them some idea as to how you see this idea ending up**

The idea will revolutionise the fast-food/home delivery industry by proving that gourmet meals can be sold piping hot. The idea will also feed a million bleary-eyed office workers good-quality food.

Linear storytelling is all about practising your story and keeping your audience glued to their seats. It takes lots of practise but that's what bringing a good idea to life is all about.

Being a good storyteller in the twenty-first century will be one of the most highly sought after skills. A good story keeps your audience interested, animated, intrigued – and attentive to the end.

It is very true that a great idea badly told is much harder to sell than a good idea well told.

Practise storytelling your idea in a room by yourself. Use a tape recorder to record the way you sound.

Ask yourself these five important questions:
- Does your story sound compelling?
- Does it follow a logical narrative path?
- Does it leave you wanting to hear more?
- Does it sound like a simple and obvious (yet brilliant) idea?
- Is it an idea your audience will be able to clearly visualise?

Another way to approach the issue of storytelling is to find a partner who can sell your idea for you. If you honestly feel that your strength is in the area of creativity rather than of selling, you can find a partner who is expert in telling your story.

However you approach the telling of your 'story', you need to be certain about one thing. *Linear* storytelling is the key. If you can convey your idea in a logical, entertaining fashion, you will give your idea the best chance it has to survive.

Step 16:
Setting the Bait

Setting the bait is all about packaging your idea in a way that whets the appetite of your audience and captures their imaginations – to the point where they can close the circle themselves. What do we mean by 'close the circle'?

Closing the circle is all about giving your audience the imagination they need to see the idea fully realised.

One of the best examples of recent times is the movie Blair Witch Project. This independent movie captured the spirit and soul of Hollywood. Via the marketing of the movie premise through the Blair Witch Web site, the moviemakers were able to plant the germ of an idea that allowed the film community to imagine the movie long before they were able to view the finished product in a cinema.

At Pophouse, we are big believers in setting the bait. Many a Pophouse idea has been originated through the

ideas generation

Pophouse Web site. All that existed was the germ of an idea that much larger companies were able to see the *value* in and the *potential of*.

The true value of setting the bait is that the idea becomes real in a very small (and often affordable) way. Hundreds of start-ups throughout the world have come into being through this process.

What did they do?

Pick up any business magazine – we recommend Fortune and Fast Company as two magazines that demonstrate this process in almost every issue. Instead of having an idea down on paper, take some small steps in realising it.

Let's go back to our idea of Pophouse laundry detergent. Let's say that Pophouse wants to seriously enter the laundry detergent market. Following the setting the bait step – what would we do?

Firstly, we would set ourselves a small budget. This investment we would treat as betting money – something we are able to lose if things do not go according to plan. After all, we are also business people – risk versus reward is the name of the game. We need to calculate the level of investment we feel comfortable risking.

We would probably manufacture as many boxes of laundry detergent as possible. We would approach a generic washing detergent manufacturer and a packaging manufacturer and make, say, 10,000 boxes. We would save money on design (by designing the boxes ourselves – after all, the Pophouse brand is one we created ourselves and know inside out!) and spend what limited capital we have on securing very limited distribution in whatever supermarket chain or mini-market store we could and the rest on unorthodox and cost-effective marketing (say telegraph poster wraps). We would also promote our detergent through our own Web site and distribute it there as well. We might offer distribution through other Web sites (shopfast etc) or through direct selling companies like Amway and offer them the share of profits. For the moment we are not interested in making money but in getting the idea off the ground.

But the smartest thing we would do is brand the detergent in the Pophouse way, utilising the Pophouse brand principles – **creativity, originality, knowledge and most importantly - content.**

We would examine and analyse the current detergent market and see that the category is stagnant, unimaginative and predictable.

We would utilise social trends and social forecasting to realise that the market is ready for a fun detergent that still delivers quality and excellent results.

We would then spend our time marketing the detergent in the press – through PR – and position our detergent as pop culture's answer to the menial task of washing.

It would be the New Economy version of washing detergent – a detergent for the new world we live in – one that has few boundaries, that is crazy and exciting and limitless in terms of potential. We would challenge the notions of boredom and predictability. But we would still realise the most important rule of the washing detergent category – it washes!

We would be irreverent and create meaning where there currently is none.

We would challenge the market and create some noise.

Because Pophouse is not and does not plan to be a washing detergent manufacturer, we might hope that one of three things could (potentially) happen:

ideas generation

- The detergent takes off and we offered larger distribution through the large supermarket chains.
- We get so much positive publicity and press that we scare the big manufacturers of washing detergent and they offer to buy us and close us down to keep us quiet.
- There is real merit in the idea and a major player offers to license the Pophouse brand name or enter a joint venture to take the very, very small seed of an idea and turns it into a viable business.

There are countless other possible outcomes but this example should give you an idea of why *setting the bait* or planting the seed can be such a valuable way to get your idea on a path to happening in the real world.

Think of at least three ways to set the bait using your idea.

Make sure they fit the following criteria:

- Can be realised on a limited budget.
- Is extremely strategic and clever – challenge an existing industry.
- Can gain good PR coverage for free and is some thing people will talk about.
- Is something that will not stretch your business to the point of exhaustion – both in terms of strategic and emotional pressure.

Finally, have some fun with this step. It's a great way to shake things up a little and see what opportunities come out of the woodwork.

Step 17:
It's Not Your Idea

One of the most successful ways of selling your idea is to give the credit to someone else! This may sound like a strange thing to do, but it can often make your audience more comfortable with the idea itself – and more comfortable with you, as the idea owner. Now, we're not recommending that you steal someone else's idea and present it as your own, but we are saying that you should feel comfortable about presenting your idea as an improvement on some other idea that already exists in the market place.

Let us give you an example. Recently a business associate of ours presented an idea to an international frozen food company. She had invented an easy way to open frozen food plastic bags after the bags containing frozen food had been microwaved or boiled.

The idea for a 'self-opening' bag is not new, but it is new in the frozen foods industry. She had simply taken an existing idea and applied the knowledge to design a new-patented system for extremely hot plastic bags. When the executives heard the idea, they had already been convinced that the idea was a great one and immediately offered further development money to test the patent under extreme conditions.

The point of this story is that the idea was not 100 per cent new. The application is new, the patent is unique – but the basic principles had already existed in the market place.

ideas generation

You need to ask yourself one very important question. Do you want to make the idea happen or do you want to be famous? If you answered yes to the former, then it doesn't really matter how original your idea is – except that you were the one to amend the idea and make it work in a new context. Remember – it's all about making the idea happen!

So:

- **Write down your idea in the centre of a piece of paper.**
- **Think of five ideas that already exist in the market that are similar to your idea.**
- **Write each of them down on a separate piece of paper.**
- **Now one at a time, take each of these five ideas and write down as many ways as you can think of that could be seen as being similar to your idea. Use the paper to draw any types of analogies you can think of – maps and diagrams can sometimes be helpful.**

Recently we have been involved in creating a new information product. Although our idea is technically new, is it simply a new application of an old (successful!) idea. When we did this exercise ourselves and then used those similarities when presenting the idea to prospective business partners, our audience was far readier to believe that our idea was a good one – and could be profitable for their business.

Another important point you need to remember is that your audience may not possess the greatest of creative minds. In order for them to visualise the idea they may need some help. If they have something to focus on, some idea to use as a reference point, your selling job may be just that much easier.

Remember – the name of the game is communication. You need to be able to clearly communicate your idea to your audience – and to achieve this objective you need to do whatever it takes.

Analogies and case studies are excellent ways for you to strengthen the proof of your own idea and to offer evidence of potential success. There in no shame is utilising somebody else's pathway to success. Through the process you will learn an enormous amount about your own idea and skills of selling your idea to your audience.

Step 18:
Shopping it Around

'Shopping it around' can be a high-risk strategy but if done (and played) correctly, it can be wonderfully advantageous to your idea. Again, remember that the objective of the game is to see your ideas realised.

'Shopping it around' is all about offering your idea to two or three competing companies and leveraging each company's potential interest against the other.

It is about creating as much interest in your idea as you possibly can. The funny thing about potentially good ideas is that when one company believes that another company might be interested in that idea, they tend to become interested too.

ideas generation

All's fair in love and ideas!

As an ideas generator, you want to give your idea the absolute best shot at survival. You are well within your rights to shop your idea around. Obviously, you need to cover yourself legally (we'll cover this in Step 21 as well as in Chapter 10) but you should not feel restrained by speaking to only one investor or venture capitalist or company. One company may promise you something but as long as you are within your rights legally, there should be nothing stopping you from seeking somebody else's opinion as well. The ideal situation you want to create is one where you bring as many people to the discussion table as possible.

Another great advantage of shopping your idea around is that you become much better at telling your story. With practice comes not only much greater self-confidence but a much tighter and more refined version of the storytelling process. You become far better at reading your audience, tweaking your 'sell' and understanding the finely tuned nuances of business. As your confidence grows, you are able to better distinguish between the pleasantries and the real opportunities – the fakes and the people who really do have the power to make a deal.

Importantly, you also develop a thick skin and improve on the business of relationships; as one of our greatest mentors says, "Business is about relationships".

Perhaps the greatest thing about shopping your idea around is that you learn the importance of keeping your cards close to your chest and only speaking about the things you want to speak about, rather than what your audience thinks you need to disclose to them.

Selling an idea doesn't mean you have to disclose every single detail of your life – on the contrary, a little mystery can go a long way in closing the deal. If you shop the idea around, you have a better chance of maintaining your independence in the idea-selling phase of development rather than feeling indebted to every person to whom you open your mouth.

The more personal and professional power you maintain, the better your chances of being taken as a serious business person, able to understand the risks (and rewards) associated with business. Because you will be exposed to all types of people, from finance to marketing to research and development, you will be forced to prepare yourself at all levels of business. If you are meeting the financial controller you will need to understand how to read spreadsheets and write up a business plan. If you are meeting the marketing director, you will need to have some idea about marketing and advertising. We're not suggesting that you need to be an expert in everything, just have an appreciation for the discipline and understand what it takes to get an idea off the ground.

Finally, if your idea does have merit, it is better to have a couple of potential investors rather than one; you don't want to regret showing your idea to the first person you approached. Remember, nothing ventured, nothing gained.

On the downside, you do not want to alienate a genuinely potential investor who may feel you are playing games. That is why it is extremely important for you to seek the right legal information and advice. It is a balancing act: your right to show your idea to as many people as possible who show interest, with the understanding that the more people who see it, the less confidential it becomes (even with confidentiality

ideas generation

agreements) versus losing the one genuine investor who may be scared off by other players.

Think of it in terms of an auction. Sometimes the one genuine buyer stays away because they assume they are out of the running. Be careful. Shop around – but keep your wits about you!

Step 19:

Painting a Picture

Painting a picture can be seen as an extension of linear storytelling (Step 15). It is all about using every visual and audio trick you have at your disposal to build a fantastic (and convincing) picture of your idea in the real world. A picture really does tell a thousand words – particularly when your audience has not had the amount of time with the idea that you have.

Use the visual aids that will help you set the scene and build a stage from which you can let your idea shine. Think about stills, storyboards, video storyboards and any other relevant, useful aids that can speak loudly and clearly to your audience. The trick here is to make sure that the picture you paint is relevant to your story and helpful rather than cumbersome to your presentation.

Alternatively, you may decide you can paint a picture with words only. Regardless of what you decide to do, the victory will be in the preparation.

We once helped an ideas generator colleague of ours present an idea to a large airline. He had developed an idea for a new magnetic tray for serving aeroplane meals that stopped the tray from moving around. Rather than just present the prototype to the development team of the huge airline in question, we came up with the idea of simulating the experience of eating a meal whilst flying through turbulence by hiring a chair that simulated turbulence.

In his presentation, our colleague attached a tray table and his new tray invention and asked each of his audience to take turns sitting in the chair. He made his point loudly and clearly. Each of the executives was extremely impressed with the presentation. The last we heard, he was unable to talk about the project. A good sign!

Think laterally and extensively about the ways you can paint a picture to your audience. Sometimes the people signing the cheques are not the most imaginative people in the world; they may need a little nudging in the right direction – your direction.

In another example, we helped an ideas generator build a visual future of the market place after his particular idea had been in the market for one year, two years, five years and ten years. We were able to clearly demonstrate the impact and overall effect the particular idea had on the market. We can't talk about this idea, but suffice to say that the audience thought twice about dismissing it without fully investigating its potential.

The ideas owner was able to cleverly articulate the competitive nature of the idea and we're certain he scared a few of those people in the meeting. Showing your potential competition the impact of your idea on their business can be pretty sobering. What we can report is that the idea was sold and a fee agreed and the product will make it to market in the next eighteen months.

A word of caution here. Your idea needs to stand up to scrutiny without the window dressing. A great visual

ideas generation

aid cannot make an average idea great. Before you even start thinking about using visual aids, go back to Steps 8–14 (spotting the great ideas from the not so great). Make sure that you are only enhancing the presentation of your idea rather than attempting to compensate for an average idea. Watching a presentation that is all style and no substance is a very painful lesson to learn for the ideas generator. Remember that painting a picture is all about telling the story and not about "poly-gripping" a badly thought-out idea.

The great advantage of this step is to give your idea the last onceover before you start to shop it around. Often, in this window dressing stage, ideas generators find out that they really don't have a compelling idea and it might be better to go back to the drawing board.

Either way, it is a fantastic process for you to use.

Paint away!

Step 20:

Batting Away Objections

Any good businessperson will shoot an idea down before even starting to think about the possibilities.

Why?

Because that's good business. Why let the idea owner believe that they have something worthwhile on their hands? Better to make them sweat it out and fight for every piece of recognition. Tough but true.

Shooting down an idea from the point of view of your audience can achieve a number of things. It can test your mettle and your commitment, it can flush you out if you are faking your knowledge of the industry or category, it can test your legal knowledge and it can bring down the price of your idea.

Learning how to bat away objections is one of the best lessons you can learn. It may take some time, but once you've mastered the art, it is a skill that can help you in countless business (and even personal) situations.

What you must do before you even present your idea to anybody is to train yourself in the combat of rejection. Because that's exactly what batting away is – combat. It's about learning how to keep your idea alive, even when your audience is telling you it can't be done.

Rule Number One: Defence

Work out and write down the top five reasons why somebody would say 'no' to your idea.

Have an answer prepared for each of the reasons.

For example, Pophouse presents its idea for Pophouse laundry detergent to a major laundry detergent manufacturer. The audience gives us five reasons why it won't work.

- You have no credibility in the detergent market.
- You have no expertise in the making the product itself.
- The Pophouse brand is too creative for the detergent category.
- No one will give you distribution.
- You do not have the money needed for such a large job – distribution, marketing, R&D.

We have already thought of the answers *to bat away each of these objections.*

- We don't need to – our consumer trends projections tell us that they are ready to try any new brand – as long as it can deliver the quality. There is no loyalty to brands in the washing detergent category, including the brands that you sell.
- We don't need any expertise. A generic manufacturer is making the product for us. By the way, they are the same company that makes some of your generic brands for you.
- The Pophouse brand is perfect for the washing detergent category in the same way that Virgin was great for the airline category. Washing detergent is boring and predictable. Pophouse Concentrated will be the biggest news the category has had for ages.
- We have already landed the Woolworths account. They are willing to give us a go as long as we shift product.
- All our money has gone into PR – we made the cover of three major magazines, 60 Minutes is doing a story on us, as are all the retail magazines. Because it's such a pop culture story, we have been given lots of coverage. We estimate that the coverage amounts to roughly $4 million of advertising. That's the combined total of all of your advertised brands put together.

Rule Number Two: Do the numbers
Money is the greatest stumbling block in the history of ideas generation. How much will it cost, when can we see a return on our investment, how large is the risk, what damage could it do to our bottom line?

You need to do the numbers – even if they are rough. You must demonstrate that you have a good working knowledge of money – how to make it and how to protect it.

Your audience will throw figures at you for what will seem like an eternity. You need to know whether they are telling the truth or scaring you off. All potential investors will throw any type of curve ball at you they can to see if you have done your homework. We have only one suggestion: Do your homework!

Batting away objections is all about preparation. Think about all of the pitfalls before they occur. Find answers to negative questions – any questions. Be harder on yourself than any inquisition could be.

We'll say it again. Do your homework!

Step 21:

Doing the Deal

If you've come this far you deserve a medal. But before you crack open the champagne to celebrate, be careful. Many deals have been known to fall down at the last minute.

Before you even hear what your audience/potential partner or investor has to say, get representation. Do not even open your mouth without legal counsel. Don't even think about it.

In Chapter 10 we will spend some more time going through some of the key legal issues in more depth, but for now, remember your place in the process. You generated the idea. You are not a lawyer. It is not personal. It's business. Do not get emotional.

You've done your job – now let your lawyers do theirs.
There will numerous ways that the venture can progress.

In legal negotiations, there is often a great deal of going back and forth. Don't be concerned if things take a while to happen.

Work out what you really want
You need to think about want you really want, really clearly. What is it you are searching for? Seeing this single idea turn into a long-term career, gaining respect and the reputation to follow, an ideas track record, or money? If you can work out what you most seek, then you can advise your legal counsel who can work towards getting you exactly what you want.

Although we've said that you should let your legal counsel do his or her job, you need to give advice about the best way to proceed. For example, if it is money you seek, your lawyer/s need to fight for as much money as possible. If it is a long-term career you seek, then your lawyers may recommend you take less money up-front with more of a view to the longer term.

Don't lose your cool at the eleventh hour
It's not done until it's done. Until the agreement is signed, numerous things can go wrong. We don't mention this to scare you but to remind you that every idea has the capacity to become high stakes business.

Take each step of the negotiations one step at a time. Don't let greed get in your way.

9

Using the Internet as an ideas tool

Online research and marketing resources.

In a recent poll of 1200 Internet users the biggest complaint was the lack of good navigational tools. Sixty-five per cent of respondents claimed that they gave up the search before they had found exactly what they were looking for. With this information in mind, we have created a chapter that acts as the ultimate Internet guide for ideas generators.

In this chapter it is our intention to do as much of the work for you as we can in terms of online research. We have been using the Internet as an ideas resource since its commercialisation in 1991 and over the last ten years we have come across a great number of valuable sites designed to assist in the development and evaluation of ideas. We believe that the more crevices you look under, the more creative you become.

Throughout this chapter there are handy lists of recommended sites that we have collected and utilised in

ideas generation

our own creative journey. Most of the sites contain links to other sites, inventors' chat rooms and ideas magazines, so don't forget to click through all of the links once you are online!

A word of warning: These lists do not constitute a formal recommendation for any specific company or individual. Rather they are intended as a catalogue designed to save you time. We would also caution that, whilst there are many online organisations genuine in their efforts to assist the individual, we have encountered many that are not. When engaging any third party in your project we always recommend that you obtain references from past clients in order to understand the nature and ultimate price of the assistance on offer. Be aware also that some sites may cease to exist just as new sites are always being developed.

The Ultimate Online Resources List

General

During the course of building Pophouse, we have come across many useful websites. Here is a selection of websites which have helped us to evaluate our ideas and have provided us with tips on protection of our ideas.

Check out two innovative sites at www.patentideas.com and www.tenonline.org – both provide a unique perspective on the evaluations and legal processes. They are American sites but they give you a good idea of grassroots level ideas communities in the US.

Another interesting US site is the IBM Intellectual Property Network (IPN). This is a premier Web site for searching, viewing and analysing patent documents.

The IPN provides you with free access to a wide variety of data collections and patent information including:

- United States patents
- European patents and patent applications
- PCT application data from the World Intellectual Property Office
- Patent Abstracts of Japan
- IBM Technical Disclosure Bulletins

Searching is easy. Along with simple keyword search, IPN offers alternative searches by patent number, boolean text, and advanced text that allows for multiple field searching. Browsing provides an organised approach to searching for patents. Through a review of specific classifications, you can identify topics and patents of interest.

- All collections are cross-referenced and forward and backward linked to all other referencing documents for immediate access to related information.
- The IPN also offers access to value added and third party services on a fee basis. The IPN is e-commerce enabled to allow immediate electronic delivery of many services.

Check out the IPN at:www.patents.ibm.com

ideas generation

Sites to help keep kids creative and inventive

Check these sites out for some dynamic activities based on inventions and their inventors if you want your kids to get more creative and inventive. All of these resources are especially great for teachers. They are also good for you too as they may help to bring out the child in you and get your creative juices flowing.

adventure.com
kidspace.com
ajkids.com
kids-korner.com
kidsdomain.com
pbs.org/kids
toonacat.com
thecase.com/kids
kidscastle.si.edu
eduplace.com

See also:
totcity.com
vrusa.com
realkids.com
haringkids.com
kidsdigreed.com
sparky.org
dek-d.com

Important US ideas sites

We have selected the following websites because they can help you answer some of the tough questions. They can provide research and financial data to either support or refute your idea.

Globus and NTDB www.stat-usa.gov/tradtest.nsf
Site for the US business, economic and trade community, providing authoritative information from the federal government. Access this area for current and historical trade-related releases, international market research, trade opportunities, country analysis, and trade library, the National Trade Data Bank (NTDB).

Library of Congress http://lcweb.loc.gov
Reading rooms online for researchers. African and Middle Eastern, Asian, business reference, European, geography and maps, Hispanic, law library, newspapers and current periodicals, science and technology.

Mega search at Brainwave www.n2kbrainwave.com
Although this is not a true intellectual property search site, it is fabulous for researching news, financial data, industry trends, Dunn & Bradstreet reports and a literal cornucopia of company or industry data. It's a 'pay as you go' site that allows you to charge to your credit card, with most reports under 50¢ to search, and $5 to download the complete report. We can't praise this site sufficiently as a market research aid.

ideas generation

Kopel Research Group Inc. www.kopel.com
Performs new product research and can market test your product. Research techniques include qualitative focus groups, mall intercept surveys, telephone surveys, mail surveys and now introducing email and Web-based surveys on the Internet.

Intellectual Property Valuations and Marketing
http://valuationcorp.com
Intellectual Property Valuations including market research, position testing, licence consulting and valuation services on all forms of intellectual property.

McGlothin Marketing www.marketfactory.com
McGlothlin Marketing helps small and mid-sized businesses answer tough marketing questions. They specialise in commercial and industrial marketing in North America. They identify market and development programs, as well as testing product concepts and identifying market potential.

Competitive Research www.companiesonline.com
Companies Online has a terrific database with millions of companies – search for competitive information.

Law Research www.lawresearch.com
Some good legal opinions and research of interest to the small business. Updated frequently, so keep checking for new reports.

US Census Bureau www.census.gov
Viewable: Every Census Bureau publication since 1 January 1996. Includes foreign population characteristics.

US International Trade Administration
www.ita.doc.gov
This page links to ITA Web sites that provide coverage of key industrial and services clusters, organised as follows: Technology and Aerospace, Tourism, Basic Industries, Environmental Technologies, Service Industries and Finance, and Textiles-Apparel and Consumer Goods.

World News Connection http://worldtec.fedworld.gov/
Sponsored by NTIS. Quick and easy location of time-sensitive world news including newspaper articles, conference proceedings, television and radio broadcasts, periodicals and non-classified technical reports, within 48–72 hours of original publication or broadcast, from Central Eurasia, East Asia, Near East and South Asia, China, East Europe, West Europe, Latin America, sub-Saharan Africa.

State of the Nation http://domino.stat-usa.gov/
Access this area for current and historical economic and financial releases and economic data. Stay informed with direct access to the federal government's wealth of information on the US economy. Access to files for subscribers only. ($50 for three-month subscription.)

Biz Library www.biz-lib.com
More than 150 industry segments can be searched online for free. Get reports on: aviation and marine, UK consumer markets, business and industry, communications and technology, construction, energy, healthcare, investment and finance, legal, media, regional markets.

ideas generation

Companies Online Competitive Research
www.companiesonline.com
Companies Online has a terrific database with millions of companies - search for competitive information.

Cyber Atlas www.cyberatlas.com
The demographic results shown are the primary results of the Baruch College – Harris Poll commissioned by Business Week. Market size, Web demographics, usage patterns and more – if you are intending to market on the Web.

Electric Library www.elibrary.com/search.cgi
Provides multiple search features to allow you immediate and access to hundreds of full-text magazines and newspapers, along with news wires, books, transcripts and thousands of pictures and maps.

Hoovers Online www.hoovers.com
One of the most comprehensive and deepest company search resources available. Primarily for publicly traded companies.

Industry Classification Index www.sematech.org
These codes allow you to target specific industry segments, before beginning your research. Identify your and your competitor's NAICS and SIC codes - then add this information to your D&B or other search.

Industry Research Desk www.virtualpet.com
One of the most comprehensive market research sites we have seen anywhere - detailed, up to date, provides more research information then you could want.

Knowledge Express www3.knowledgeexpress.com
Instantly search across all resources at Knowledge Express and view results with just one request. Research new product development concepts. Target recent university/corporate/government licensable technologies and locate potential business and funding sources. Powerful, focused, provides well-screened results.

Lexis-Nexis www.lexis-nexis.com
Information is easily organised so you can search on people, products and companies. LEXIS-NEXIS reQUESTer is an ideal tool for marketing information, and for locating marketing strategies, public relations and advertising information as well as legal/industry/financial/company/news information. Fee-based – used by the pros.

Market Stats www.marketstats.com
Provides ready-made online charts, graphs and data on a variety of economic and government indicators to help with your market research data development.

Research Link www.researchlink.com
Market research, industrial research, corporate research, virtual research. They offer trade linking services as well as virtual marketing packages

Standard Rate Data Services www.srds.com
Resource for demographic research data based on subscriptions of every magazine sold in the United States including business publications, consumer magazines, newspapers, direct marketing lists, radio, TV and cable and out-of-home.

ideas generation

Financing sites

These websites will provide you with information regarding potential financing opportunities for your ideas.

TRW Credit Reporting www.creditreports.com
Investigate any US corporation you are considering doing business with for $49.95. Online ordering and online report delivery – fast.

THA Capital Connection
www.capital-connection.com
Helps entrepreneurs and businesses find capital. Free newsletter. Join FIND, a moderated discussion list on the challenges of finance and entrepreneurs if you're looking for venture capital business planning information.

Venture Financing Resource Directory
www.vfinance.com
Plug into venture capitalists galore (as well as investment banking firms and commercial credit companies); many listed by preferred industry.

Financing Resources www.financingsources.com
For loans and venture capital, this may be your answer. If you leave Datamerge with unanswered questions, maybe you really don't need funding.

America's Business Funding Directory
www.businessfinance.com
This free resource allows you to input your financing needs, and get a customised listing and contact information

of funding resources (from over 15,000 listed) matching your needs.

Biz Dot www.biz-dot.com
Resources, services and software to help start-ups and expanding businesses get private investment funding. Info on Reg. D, 504, 505 and 506 offerings, SCOR, limited partnerships and more.

Commventure Partners www.commventure.com
Specialising in very early stage companies – this venture firm invests only in wireless communication technology companies.

Finance Hub http://FinanceHub.com
100 venture capital sites (free search), over 200 banks in five categories – a cornucopia of funding possibilities for your project/company

Capital Search Engine www.businessfinance.com
Download free resource A library of business resources. about foreign trade, government information, tips for travellers, business education, helpful associations, and more.

Jade Research www.win-sbir.com
A leading firm in the provision of resources to the SBIR and STTR communities, providing current, up-to-date news covering all agencies of the SBIR and STTR programs.

Money Hunter www.moneyhunter.com
Entrepreneur's weekly e-zine with business plan templates and information from the American public TV

ideas generation

program Money Hunt. Money Hunter features small businesses seeking funding on their PBS TV program, but you need to submit your plan well in advance

SBA Small Business Loans
http://www.sba.gov
The 7(a) Loan Guaranty Program is one of SBA's primary lending programs

University of Arkansas www.ualr.edu
Well indexed listing of numerous business articles online including sections on venture capital, patents, trademarks and copyrights - a wealth of information!

Small Business Research
www.acq.osd.mil/sadbu/sbir
Latest list of technology and product development projects for which the SBIR is looking for proposals.

Venture Capital Forums
http://forum.capital-connection.com
New venture capital forum provides a place to post or read information on business plans, venture capital, other forms of funding, finding finance professionals, and more – on six different forums.

Business Incubation Service www.nbia.org
Business incubation is a dynamic process of business enterprise development. Incubators nurture young firms, helping them to survive and grow during the startup period when they are most vulnerable. Incubators provide hands-on management assistance, access to financing and orchestrated exposure to critical business or technical

support services. They also offer entrepreneurial firms shared office services, access to equipment, flexible leases and expandable space – all under one roof.

An incubation program's main goal is to produce successful graduates – businesses that are financially viable and freestanding when they leave the incubator, usually in two to three years. Thirty percent of incubator clients typically graduate each year. According to the Impact of Incubator Investments Study, 1997, 87% of incubator graduates are still in business.

Like venture capitalists, incubators impose selection criteria upon prospective clients. Some accept a mix of industries, but others concentrate on industry niches. According to NBIA research, incubator clients may be classified as follows:
- 43% Mixed Use
- 25% Technology
- 10% Manufacturing
- 9% Targeted**
- 6% Service
- 5% Empowerment
- 2% Other

**Targeted incubators focus on assisting start-up companies from a specific industry, such as biomedical, wood products, arts, food production, fashion, etc.

The businesses being incubated today are at the forefront of developing new and innovative technologies – creating products and services that improve the quality of our lives – on a small scale today, and on a much grander scale tomorrow.

The National Business Incubation Association is a private, not-for-profit 501(c)(3) membership organization with headquarters in Athens, Ohio. The Association is

ideas generation

governed by an elected fifteen-member voting Board of Directors representing leading incubators.

International Incubator Locations

Australia www.ozemail.com.au/~anzabi
Belgium www.anprotec.org.br
Brazil www.anprotec.org.br
Canada http://strategis.ic.gc.ca
Finland http://com.utu.fi/techcenter
Germany www.adt-online.de
Israel http://news.incubators.org.il
United Nations www.unido.org
United Kingdom www.ukbi.co.uk

Regional US Business Incubator Locations

We have provided you with a list of US contact details in case you are developing an idea for a global market. It may be helpful to know whether your idea or trademark already exists overseas.

Alabama
Alabama Business Incubation Network
Ten Incubator Locations throughout Alabama. Shoals Entrepreneurial Center, 3115 Northington Court, Florence, AL 35630, t: (205) 760-9014, f: (205) 740-5530
Birmingham Business Assistance Network
110 12th Street North, Birmingham, Alabama 35203, t: (205)250-8000, f: (205)250-8013
Office for the Advancement of Developing Industries
2800 Milan Court, Birmingham, Alabama 35211, t: (205) 943-6560, f: (205) 943-6563

9 Using the Internet as an ideas tool

Montgomery Incubator
600 South Court Street, P.O. Box 79, Montgomery, AL 36101,
t: (334) 240-6863, f: (334) 240-6869

Arkansas
Genesis Technology Incubator
University of Arkansas, 700 West 20th Street, Fayetteville, AR 72701-8362, t: (501) 575-7227, f: (501) 575-7446

Arizona
Arizona Technology Incubator
1435 North Hayden Road, Scottsdale, Arizona 85257-3773,
t: (602) 990-0400, f: (602) 970-6355

California
Access Capital Organization
Strong medicine for the technology entrepreneur. Sacramento area based, mentoring. Site also has tons of useful, timely information on Venture Capital and technology transfer.
CALSTART Business Hatchery
Southern California Office: 3601 Empire Avenue, Burbank, CA 91505,
 t: (818) 565-5600
Business Cluster Development
160 N. Castanya, Menlo Park, CA 94028, t: (650) 854-1707
Communications Technology Cluster (CTC)
2201 Broadway, 2nd Floor, Oakland, CA 94612-1932, t: (510) 836-8985,
f: (510) 836-8987
San Diego Enterprise Center
10401 Roselle Street, Suite 200, San Diego, CA 92121, t: 619-587-9974,
f: 619-587-9976
Center for Applied Competitive Technologies
San Diego City College, 1313 Twelfth Ave, San Diego, CA 92101,
t: (619) 230-2080, f: (619) 230-2162

ideas generation

International Business Incubator
111 North Market Street, Suite 610, San Jose, California 95113-1101,
t: (408) 288-6120, f: (408) 288-6123

Georgia
Advanced Technology Development
10th Street430 Tenth Street Suite N-116, Atlanta, GA 30318,
t: (404) 894-3575, f: (404) 894-4545
Southeastern Technology Center
501 Greene Street, Suite 400, Augusta, Georgia 30901,
t: (706) 722-3490, f: (706) 722-4524

Hawaii
Manoa Innovation Center (MIC)
2800 Woodlawn Drive, Suite 100, Honolulu, Hawaii 96822,
t: (808) 539-3600, f: (808) 539-3611

Idaho
North Central Idaho Business Technology Incubator
121 Sweet Avenue, Moscow, ID 83843, t: (208) 885-3801
Bonner Business Center
804 Airport Way, Sandpoint, ID 83864, t: (208) 263-4073,
f: (208) 263-4609
CSI Business Incubator
College of Southern Idaho, 315 Falls Avenue, P.O. Box 1238, Twin Falls,
ID 83303-1238, t: (208) 733-9554 Ex. 2450, f: (208) 733-9316

Illinois
The Chicago Southland Enterprise Center
1655 Union, Chicago Heights, Illinois, t: (708) 754-6960,
f: (708) 754-8779
Small Business Development Center
Office of Economic and Regional Development, Southern Illinois

University, Carbondale, IL 62901, (618) 536-2424, f: (618) 453-5040
Northwestern University/Evanston Research Park
820 Church Street, Suite 300
Evanston, Illinois 60201, t: (847) 475-7170, f: (847) 475-7380
Technology Commercialization Laboratory
2004 South Wright Street Extended, Urbana, IL 61802, Campus Mail Code 710, t: 217-244-7742, f: 217-244-7757

Indiana
Entrepreneur Business Center
55 S. State Ave., Indianapolis, IN 46201, t: (317) 236-0143

Louisiana
Louisiana Business Incubator Association (LBIA)
Enterprise Center of Louisiana 3419 N.W. Evangeline Thruway, Carencro, LA 70520, t: (318) 896-9115, f: (318) 896-8736
Louisiana Business & Technology Center
Louisiana State University, South Stadium Drive, Baton Rouge, LA 70803-6100, t: (225) 334-5555

Maryland
Technology Advancement Program
335 Paint Branch Drive, University of Maryland, College Park, MD 20742, t: (301) 314-7803, f: (301) 314-9592
Rural Development Center
Richard A. Henson Center, Room 2147, UMES, Princess Anne, MD 21853, t: (410) 651-6183, f: (410) 651-6207

Massachusetts
Massachusetts Innovation Center
One Oak Hill Road, Fitchburg, Massachusetts 01420, t: (978) 342-0101
Enterprise Center at Salem State College, 352 Lafayette Street, Salem, MA 01970, t: (978) 542-7528, f: (978) 542-8387

ideas generation

Michigan
MBI International
P.O. Box 27609, Lansing, MI 48909-0609, t: 517-337-3181

Minnesota
Genesis Business Centers, Ltd.
3989 Central Ave. N.E., Suite 530, Columbia Heights, MN 55421,
t: (612) 782-8576, f: (612)782-8578

Missouri
St. Louis County Economic Council
Suite 900, 121 South Meramec, St. Louis, Missouri 63105

Texas
Texas Business Incubator Association
c/o E.D.C. 8845 Long Pt. Road, Houston, TX 77055-3019,
t: (713) 932-7495, x13, f: (713) 932-7498

Twenty-two sites we love

These sites are regularly visited by Pophouse staff.

www.garage.com
Garage.com helps entrepreneurs and investors build great businesses.

For entrepreneurs, Garage.com provides assistance in obtaining seed level financing as their number one objective. They compress the entrepreneur's 'time-to-money' via mentoring and a high-quality investor network, thus allowing the entrepreneur to focus more time building his or her business.

They also provide member entrepreneurs with expert advice, research and reference materials, and topical Forums to help them launch and grow their startup.

For investors, they identify and provide pre-screened, high-quality investment opportunities that match the investor's identified interests. These opportunities are presented in a uniform format that helps investors evaluate companies quickly and easily.

Additionally, members have access to a broad community of investors focused on the cutting edge of high technology, enabling them to work together as they identify and qualify investment opportunities.

www.patentsonline.com.au
Platonic Hood Patents on Line Australia is a NSW-registered partnership business name, with ABN U2024337, and is tailored to provide online consulting services on intellectual property matters for small/medium-sized businesses and individuals. The same name is associated

with a logo in a original graphic representation, and registered as trademark which can be also identified through its number: 708120.

Platonic Hood Patents on Line Australia's primary services include patent, trademark and design searching, maintenance, technical support and watching services provided by engineering representatives and professionals in chemistry, physics, mining, electronics, mechanics, civil engineering and computer systems.

Platonic Hood Patents on Line Australia's goal is to apply customer-focused logistics by understanding the needs and value of each customer or client's class and to design and deliver distinct bundles of logistics services. These specialised services are designed to be comprehensive, efficient, accurate, timely, and competitively priced.

Their main categories of customers are individual inventors, patent attorneys and agents, business people, researchers, competitive-intelligence analysts, entrepreneurs, students, historians, and the general public.

www.european-patent-office.org

The European Patent Organisation was established by the Convention on the Grant of European Patents (EPC) signed in Munich in 1973, the EPO is the outcome of the European countries' collective political determination to establish a uniform patent system in Europe.

As a centralised patent grant system administered by the European Patent Office on behalf of all contracting states, it is a model of successful co-operation in Europe.

The European Patent Organisation consists of its legislative body, the Administrative Council and its executive body, the European Patent Office.

www.svbank.com

Silicon Valley Bank has launched an online resource portal for emerging, high growth clients of the bank. This offering is eSOURCE™, a web-based information center. eSOURCE provides Bank clients with the tools to alleviate their business infrastructure challenges and assist them in planning for future growth and success. The eSOURCE team has assembled a content-rich site with a continually increasing number of 'high-calibre' vendors of products and services. eSOURCE provides Silicon Valley Bank clients and prospects with business solutions specifically tailored for their industry, geography and stage of development. eSOURCE visitors frequently request introductions to the various vendors through an online 'Introduce Me' function, and become part of a community with whom they can exchange ideas and information.

www.em.asx.com.au

The enterprise market is the Australian Stock Exchange's online market which helps non-listed businesses raise capital.

The enterprise market provides investors and advisers with information about investment opportunities that exist in small, medium-sized and emerging growth businesses in Australia.

Information about the companies' background, vision, objectives, market information, management team, products, services and risks is automatically presented to the enterprise market subscribers to whom the investment opportunities are attractive.

The benefit to the businesses is that their investment proposal can reach literally thousands of potential investors at a fraction of the cost of preparing a prospectus. The enterprise market is the new Australian on-line market which brings together companies offering investment opportunities, potential investors and the business networks of hundreds of advisers.

www.tinshed.com
TiNSHED Corporation, formed in June 1999, is home to the TiNSHED Angels – Australia's first high-tech angel investment group. The TiNSHED Angels provide ventures from the Internet, media and telecommunications industries with early stage capital ($0.5–3.0m), contacts and experience.

The Corporation is also made up of a group of ten leading Australian businessmen. The TiNSHED Founding Angels are Rodney Adler, Michael Ball, Jack Cowin, John David, Will Liley, David Lowy, Robert McLean, James Packer, John Singleton and Kevin Weldon.

The term 'angel' was originally used to describe a person who aids or supports with influence or money. In a modern sense, it refers to investors who support young businesses in the earliest stages.

By banding together, angel investors are able to pool their resources, reduce personal risk and raise more capital for potential new companies.

As individuals, angels are often able to move faster and with more flexibility than institutional funds. As such, angel investment groups are becoming an increasingly attractive route for entrepreneurs seeking funding.

A TiNSHED angel is a high net worth individual who has succeeded in their industry at the highest level and is personally interested in supporting high-tech ventures. Through their depth of business knowledge, industry expertise, network of contacts and capital base, TiNSHED angels are able to add extraordinary value at the formative stages of a business, thus increasing the chances that the business will succeed.

TiNSHED introduces to Australia a hybrid of the successful US angel investment model. The corporation will not only bridge the sourcing, quality control and funding gap between start-up financing and institutional investment, TiNSHED also has the capacity to participate in subsequent rounds of funding through its multi-billion dollar shareholders and its own capital base.

TiNSHED will complement its shareholder network by developing partnerships with domestic and international industry players such as other angel groups, venture capital firms, government, high-tech corporations and technology-focused service providers.

TiNSHED is currently establishing a comprehensive network which will incorporate the major high-tech centres around the globe including Silicon Valley, Boston, Tel Aviv, Berlin, Dublin, Stockholm, Singapore and Hong Kong.

www.score.org
SCORE (Service Corps of Retired Executives) is an SBA program under which retired businesspeople offer free counselling to start-ups and small businesses. SCORE has been a mixed bag for most users for two reasons: the counselling is typically by appointment and physical visit to their office (requiring time and travel), and the counselling is typically done by whoever happens to be manning the office that day (who may or may not have the answers you're seeking). Their new Cyber Chapter bypasses both these problems. Here you can find several

ideas generation

hundred SCORE counsellors willing to counsel by e-mail – and they're listed with their areas of expertise so you know who to approach.

www.businessfinance.com

America's Business Funding Directory is the best site we've found for those seeking business capital. Over 13,000 funding sources and growing – and totally free. Enter your funding needs and they instantly show you the funding sources most likely to meet your needs – with all the info you need to contact them! What we especially like about this site is that they've gone to great lengths to help you precisely define your needs – obviously, the better you define your needs the better your odds of finding the sources that will accommodate them. While you're there, download their excellent Funding Guide workbook, *Raising Money*. Once you've found your sources, these are the kind of questions you're going to be asked – be prepared! Note: This site does not include the private investors, or angels. You'll still have to look elsewhere for them.

www.ibm.com/patents

Free patent searching courtesy of IBM. This is the same database used by IBM researchers. It currently contains text back to 1974 and full-images back to 1980 – with well-explained, easy-to-use and very versatile search facilities.

www.ideainternational.com.au

Idea International is an organisation of inventors for inventors. For more than five years they have been fine-tuning the structural and methodological foundations necessary to assess and assist in the commercialisation of new ideas.

www.uspto.gov
The site of the US Patent and Trademark Office (PTO) For over 200 years, the basic role of the US Patent and Trademark Office (PTO) has remained the same: to promote the progress of science and the useful arts by securing for limited times to inventors the exclusive right to their respective discoveries (Article 1, Section 8 of the United States Constitution). Under this system of protection, American industry has flourished. New products have been invented, new uses for old ones discovered, and employment opportunities created for millions of Americans. The PTO is a non-commercial federal entity and one of 14 bureaus in the Department of Commerce (DOC). The office occupies numerous buildings in Arlington, Virginia. The office employs over 5000 full time equivalent (FTE) staff to support its major functions – the examination and issuance of patents and the examination and registration of trademarks.

The PTO has evolved into a unique government agency. Since 1991 – under the Omnibus Budget Reconciliation Act (OBRA) of 1990 – the PTO has operated in much the same way as a private business, providing valued products and services to customers in exchange for fees which are used to fully fund operations. The primary services they provide include processing patents and trademarks and disseminating patent and trademark information.

Through the issuance of patents, they encourage technological advancement by providing incentives to invent, invest in, and disclose new technology worldwide.

ideas generation

Through the registration of trademarks, they assist businesses in protecting their investments, promoting goods and services, and safeguarding consumers against confusion and deception in the marketplace. By disseminating both patent and trademark information, they promote an understanding of intellectual property protection and facilitate the developments and sharing of new technologies world wide.

http://www.apec.org
APEC was formed in 1989 and promotes open trade and practical economic cooperation among its 18 member economies.

http://www.cpvo.fr/
The Community Plant Variety Office (CPVO) is a community organisation that implements and applies the European system for protecting plant variety rights. Their site provides information on procedures for plant variety protection, and issues such as the relationship between community and national protection.

www.ficpi.org
FICPI, the International Federation of Industrial Property Attorneys, aims to enhance international co-operation and promote business relations between its members. The site provides information on the structure and membership of the Federation and their current work around the world.

www.inventnet.com
The Inventors Network is a non-profit organisation based in the US, which provides independent inventors

with information to help them develop and market their invention.

www.jpo-miti.go.jp
This IP Information Mall is managed by the Japanese Patent Office. It provides a topical guide to the information supplied by each IP Office with direct links to the relevant area in each site.

www.lawasia.asn.au/
Lawasia (The Law Association for Asia and the Pacific) is a professional association for representatives of Law Associations, individual lawyers, law firms and corporations from the Asia Pacific region. Their site includes a section on intellectual property information.

www.rjriley.com
This Inventor Resources site has lots of useful resources for inventors of all ages, including basic hints for beginners, and more comprehensive information on commercialising your invention.

http://web.kyoto-inet.or.jp
Trade Marks in Japan outlines the current trade marks system in Japan, including information on what can be registered, how the classification system works, examination and renewal procedures.

http://www.uspto.gov
You can access the US Patent Bibliographic Database and the AIDS Patent Database from this site. Access to these databases is free of charge.

ideas generation

Legal tips

You should visit these sites regularly to keep up with any changes in intellectual property law.

Copyright

Australian Copyright Council www.copyright.org.au
An excellent online copyright information centre.

Copyright in Australia
http://law.gov.au/copyright_enews/
Intellectual Property Branch, Attorney-General's Department.

IP Branch Dept of Communication and the Arts
www.dca.gov.au
Includes an intellectual property newsletter and up-to-date information on copyright in Australia

Intellectual property laws

Australian Intellectual Property Laws
www.gtlaw.com.au
Gilbert and Tobin's quick reference guide to Australian intellectual property laws contains general material on all types of IP including brief descriptions and links for further information.

Lawpoint Website www.lawpoint.com.au
Lawpoint Website allows you to access a wide range of legal information on line.

9 Using the Internet as an ideas tool

Attorney-General's Department http://law.gov.au
This site is the entry point for all Australian government legal resources. It provides clear and understandable information about the Australian legal system and the government organisations that operate within it. You can also search their database for legal information on intellectual property.

ideas generation

Australian organisations that can assist your business

Before you rush off-shore, check for local assistance first!

Austrade (www.austrade.gov.au)

Austrade is the Australian Trade Commission – the federal government's export and investment facilitation agency. In simple terms, and to use its mission statement, they exist 'to help Australians win export business and generate inward and outward investment'.

Dialling the Export Hotline number – 13 28 78 – is the first point of contact for any business interested in exporting. Austrade's role is to help boost Australia's export earnings, so they concentrate on firms that are ready to export. The Hotline helps companies determine whether they are ready to export and provides initial advice and general market information which then helps in deciding how best to proceed.

If Austrade cannot help you, they will refer you to the appropriate government or private service who can.

Austrade Online

Austrade Online is Austrade's enhanced Web site, www.austrade.gov.au. It provides a comprehensive, up-to-date export information service, including advice on international trade issues, export programmes and overseas markets. The 'Australia on Display' section of the site is a searchable database of thousands of Australian companies and their products and services. This can be accessed by potential customers from anywhere in the world. Australian companies can take out a listing free of charge.

9 Using the Internet as an ideas tool

Entering export markets

Austrade provides advice to companies on which overseas markets hold the highest sales potential for their product, how they can build a presence in these markets, and what sort of practical and financial help is available.

Operating an international network of offices located in 108 cities in 63 countries, Austrade is able to identify potential buyers or agents and to pass on specific business opportunities as they arise. By working with Australian businesses, Austrade can accurately match Australian suppliers with interested local contacts and arrange introductions. It can also engage in long-term partnerships to ensure all possibilities are fully exploited.

Austrade provides information tailored to the specific requirements of each business. Relevant information can include detailed market intelligence such as the competition, the prospects, cultural considerations, distribution systems and government regulations. Many of Austrade's services are free or partially subsidised by the government. When the preparatory work is done, Austrade's overseas offices can contribute to a successful market visit.

Their export advisers will be able to advise you of the approximate charges that apply to the specific services you require.

In-market services

Through their global network of offices, Austrade can provide you with a range of in-market services such as setting up appointments with distributors or other useful contacts, providing on-the-spot briefing on the local business culture and environment, organising interpreters and office facilities, attending meetings to help

ideas generation

overcome language or cultural barriers, organising product launches and seminars, and preparing publicity material.

Trade fairs
International trade fairs can be an effective way of promoting your products and services to targeted buyers and users overseas. Austrade co-ordinates Australian national stands at more than 100 international trade exhibitions each year. Austrade will assist you with stand design and construction, freight forwarding and clearance, and provision of exhibitor facilities. Your business may be eligible for financial support from Austrade towards the cost of participating in trade fairs.

Financial assistance for exporters
Austrade's Export Market Development Grants (EMDG) scheme encourages Australian exporters to seek out and develop overseas markets. Under the scheme, eligible businesses are reimbursed for part of the export marketing costs they incur.

Australian Commonwealth Government
www.fed.gov.au
The entry point to accessing information about the Australian government.

Australian Securities and Investment Commission
www.asic.gov.au
ASIC is an independent government body that enforces and administers corporations law and consumer protection law for investments, life and general insurance, superannuation and banking throughout Australia.

9 Using the Internet as an ideas tool

Australian Business Ltd www.australianbusiness.com.au
Australian Business Ltd incorporates the Australian Business Chamber and the Business Services Division. They provide information on a wide range of issues such as industry policy, taxation, workplace relations, workers compensation, international trade, the environment, government procurement and labour market programs for the unemployed.
See also: http://bizlink.ausindustry.org.au/

Emerge www.emerge.com.au
EMERGE, one of six Australian co-operative multimedia centres, generates projects and initiatives to support the development of a viable multimedia industry in Victoria.

InnoMart www.innomart.com
InnoMart is the Australian inventors market place for the promotion and commercialisation of new product and intellectual property developments.

Ausinvent Innovation Services www.ausinvent.com
With the support of the New South Wales Department of State and Regional Development and a growing number of businesses and interest groups, this site provides easy access to necessary industry knowledge, and an electronic market place of innovation services.

Inventors Associations of Australia
www.magna.com.au/~iaaq/ (Queensland)
The Inventors' Association provides a forum for members to meet, exchange strategies, views and contacts. It is also a resource for professional information in the form of monthly presentations and lectures.

ideas generation

ISO QLD www.powerup.com.au (Queensland)
ISO (Queensland) provides a free service to help you identify competitive Australian companies and make the most of local content in projects and procurement. Their aim is to replace imported materials and equipment with locally manufactured products.

Sydney Business Enterprise Centre
www.sydneybec.com.au
The Sydney Business Enterprise Centre (BEC) has been established to assist the development of new and existing small businesses. They offer practical assistance and advice for your business.

Victorian Innovation Centre www.planet.net.au/~vicidea/
The Victorian Innovation Centre provides information on how to get good new products into the market place, saving you time and money. Their site also identifies a range of business opportunities in Victoria.

Intellectual Property Commission http://ipcr.gov.au
The Intellectual Property and Competition Review Committee has been established by the Australian government to review the impact of intellectual property laws on competition.

IP Menu www.ipmenu.com
This site provides a comprehensive listing of IP resources on the Internet.

The Ultimate Libraries Guide

We have included a list of weird and wonderful library sites – including places like Latvia! Often, the most off-beat net surfing can result in the most interesting ideas. Don't be afraid to look under the rocks!

National Library of Argentina www.bibnal.edu.ar
National Library of Australia www.nla.gov.au
The British Library www.bl.uk
Belgian Royal Library www.kbr.be
National Library of Canada www.nlc-bnc.ca
National Library of China www.lib.tsinghua.edu.cn/chinese/beitu
National Library of the Czech Republic www.nkp.cz
Danish National Library of Education www.dlh.dk/dpb/dpb_welcome
National Library of France www.bnf.fr
National Library of Greenland www.katak.gl
National Library of Hungary www.oszk.hu
National Library of Iceland www.bok.hi.is
National Library of Ireland www.heanet.ie/natlib
National Library of Jamaica www.nlj.org.jm
National Library of Latvia http://vip.latnet.lv/lnb/LNB_ENG
National Library of Malaysia www.pnm.my
National Library of the Netherlands www.konbib.nl
National Library of New Zealand www.natlib.govt.nz
Russian State Library www.rsl.ru
National Library of Scotland www.nls.uk
National Library of Spain www.bne.es
National Library of Sweden www.kb.se
National Library of Switzerland www.snl.ch
U.S. Library of Congress http://lcweb.loc.gov
National Library of Wales www.llgc.org.uk

10

Basic protection for your ideas

What are your intellectual property rights and what do you need to do to protect your idea?

Before we start to explain some of the ways that you can and should protect your idea legally, let's look at why protection is the most critical element of successful ideas realisation. Ideas generation is only the first step. The ultimate protection and realisation of your idea is where the real battle begins!

To understand the serious nature of protection and the potential money that a good idea can deliver, let's take two notable examples from the history of ideas protection.

Let's go back to Jerome Lemelson for a moment. Lemelson's role as a thinker is hotly debated. Critics often angrily say that he manipulated the patent system to squeeze money out of big companies. His widely accepted claim to having invented the camcorder, for

ideas generation

example, consists essentially of his theory that a handheld video camera might contain a videotape cassette on which to record pictures and sound. It can be argued that it was a novel conception. But even Lemelson makes no claim to have actually constructed such an item in the 1970s, only to having been the first to take the notion to the US Patent Office. What made his claim viable is that videotape already existed, as did portable sound recording equipment, whose design Lemelson proposed to appropriate. In such cases, the conception alone is good enough, according to the Patent Office, to merit a patent.

How much credit – and money – does Lemelson deserve for his often embryonic, conceptual efforts? This question has resulted in dozens of multimillion-dollar lawsuits.

"If you file often enough and long enough, you can eventually get a patent on almost anything," said US patent attorney Robert P. Bell, who has studied Lemelson's legal tactics. "Given sufficient time and money, I could probably get you a patent on the wheel." All it takes, he adds, is to "wear down the examiner for twenty years or so".

Lemelson's critics emphasise the enormous gap between describing an invention in words and building something that works. As the adage goes, "the devil is in the details". It takes a great deal more money to make the idea work than to have the idea in the first place.

To a large extent, Lemelson's success rested on his talent for couching his insights and innovations in the broadest possible terms. Sometimes being abstract can be extremely rewarding financially!

Lemelson's early experiences remain legendary in some technological circles. In his early days as an inventor of children's toys, he attempted to sell his ideas to toy manufacturers, only to see them copied by others. After years of believing that his ideas were being stolen, he vowed to take up the cause of independent inventors everywhere, fiercely defending his intellectual property claims. In the years that followed he came to view himself as a champion of the plight of the independent inventor – a lone David standing up to the Goliaths of the corporate world.

Lemelsons's multimillion-dollar lawsuits, led by a now-famous law firm in Nevada, won him huge settlements from some of the world's largest corporations. In one set of cases in the early 1990s he won more than $500 million from auto manufacturers and other firms for their widespread use of automated manufacturing systems that drew upon some of the machine vision patents he had initially filed decades earlier.

Despite all that time, effort, and money, though, Lemelson was forced to confront the inescapable fact that, in the hands of the legal system, even the most airtight patent claim can deflate into a worthless pile of paper. In a classic example from relatively early in his career, Lemelson won $71 million from the Mattel Company in a bitterly fought battle in which he claimed ownership of the idea behind Mattel's Hot Wheels cars and tracks. But a subsequent verdict in the court of appeals ultimately overturned the award, upholding Mattel's claim to the toy.

Solicitors routinely report an expanding pile of intellectual property battles. Intellectual property law, widely hailed as a growth area for lawyers entering the profession, already draws more young lawyers than ever before.

ideas generation

In 1997, for instance, Digital Equipment Corporation (DEC), one of the most successful computer firms, sued Intel, the world's largest computer chip maker, over rights to the $20 billion empire of Pentium chips Intel has sold to power the latest generation of computers. DEC claimed Intel stole its techniques to make the Pentium chips. Intel claimed it didn't. Finally, as part of a merger deal (with another computer giant, Compaq, gobbling up DEC), Intel purchased DEC's portfolio of relevant technology for $79 million. Who knows what to make of all of this – except that in the struggle to compete, protecting intellectual property has become as important a weapon as creating it.

In 1996, the Dow Chemical Company chartered an in-house 'intellectual-asset management' group to oversee its portfolio of 30,000-plus patents. By more aggressively charging other firms for using Dow's intellectual property assets, Dow is said to be able to enhance its 'licensing value stream' from $25 million in 1994 to a projected $125 million in the year 2000. In the future, this will be worth billions.

SmartPatents' CEO, Kevin Rivette, calls patents 'the new global currency of technology' and explains that ideas need his firm's services because intellectual property is commanding an increasing portion of what he calls 'a company's overall valuation equation'.

Example 1: The Genome Project

By now you may have heard about the Genome Project. The multibillion-dollar international effort to map the human genome presents an unprecedented opportunity. Scientists hope to have a complete map of the genome within the first decade of the new millennium.

The job of decoding, or sequencing, this genetic information is enormous.

By mapping the code that directs human cells, scientists are taking the first step toward the goal of discovering how each piece works with the others to determine human traits and characteristics. The complete genome map – which will be equivalent to roughly two hundred volumes each the size of a 1000-page telephone book – represents an essential tool to begin this research. But already private companies and academic research groups are staking exclusive claims to this vital information. Decoding the makeup, and ultimately the functioning, of the roughly one hundred thousand genes that direct cells to build human beings will revolutionise biomedical science, leading to new drugs and therapies and a deepened understanding of disease and ageing. But mapping the human genome also puts our system of ownership of knowledge assets to one of its most difficult tests: should researchers be allowed to own particular segments of the human genome they decode?

After years of equivocating, the Patent Office remains unsure whether to grant patents on this basic, preliminary information from the Human Genome Project.

A key issue is the need for open access to this information. Most information about human genes is currently being shared. At the end of 1995, one scientific team made headlines by placing on the Internet the lengthy sequence for a gene believed to be linked to breast cancer – a potentially lucrative discovery. The scientists at Washington University in St Louis and the Sanger Center in Britain said they wanted to show that such data best benefits society when it is made available freely and quickly. Since that time a wealth of genome-related

ideas generation

information has been immediately released on the Internet.

It has been estimated, however, that private firms seeking to use their genomic knowledge for commercial development are restricting that public access to at least 15 per cent of the information compiled so far.

Example 2: The Internet

The Internet began in 1969 as a project of the Pentagon's Defense Advanced Research Projects Agency (DARPA) to investigate computer networking technology. Today it has exploded into an essential infrastructure for research, education, and entertainment. In fact, it is hard to say what is more exciting: the Internet's decentralised nature or its phenomenal growth.

So far, anyone with access to a computer, a modem and a modest budget has been able to send and receive messages, as well as to read, copy, and distribute documents.

And the network is constantly growing – it is estimated that 3000 new Web sites go up every day.

Powerful Internet players have set their sights on the creation of widespread online commerce. Most analysts say that the success or failure of the Internet will hinge on the extent to which money can be made there.

But the Internet stands at a critical juncture and the key question remains – how will people protect their ideas when almost everyone can gain access to that information via the Net?

The answer to this remains to be seen.

A Toolkit for Protecting Your Ideas (Your Intellectual Property)

Well enough of the pondering, let's get down to the key ways that you as an individual ideas generator can protect yourself in the most effective ways possible.

Intellectual property represents the property of your mind or intellect. In business terms, this also means your proprietary knowledge.

Types of Intellectual Property

1. Patents

A patent is a right granted for any device, substance, method or process, which is new, inventive and useful.

A patent is legally enforceable and gives the owner the exclusive right to commercially exploit the invention for the life of the patent. This is not automatic – you have to apply for a patent. All applications for patents are examined to ensure they meet the necessary legal requirements for granting a patent.

Patents give effective protection if you have invented new technology that will lead to a product, composition or process with significant long-term commercial gain.

You cannot patent artistic creations, mathematical models, plans, schemes or other purely mental processes.

Do not go public with your invention too soon!

If you demonstrate, sell or discuss your invention in public before you file, you cannot get a patent. You can talk to employees, business partners or advisers about your invention but only on a confidential basis. Written confidentiality agreements with these people are advisable.

ideas generation

Time limit
An Australian standard patent lasts for twenty years. However, annual maintenance fees are payable from its fifth year.

Who administers patents?
Applications should be filed with the Patent Office of IP Australia. They will assess whether your invention is new and if it meets the legislative requirements.

International patents
Most countries have patent systems similar to the Australian system. Obtaining patents overseas helps you protect your valuable export markets.

Australia is party to a number of international agreements which can reduce the complexity of applying overseas. For example, the filing date of an Australian patent application can usually be used to establish priority for corresponding patent applications made overseas within the following twelve months.

Patent examples
    Bishop's Steering Gear
    Cochlear's Bionic Ear
    Dynamic Lifter
    Orbital Engine
    Hills Hoist
    Victa Lawn Mower
    Shepherd Castors
    Hume Pipes
    Automatic Totalizator
    Sunshine Stripper Harvester
    Refrigeration (in 1868)

Useful addresses
IP Australian Head Office
PO Box 200
Woden ACT 2606
National Phone Number: 1300 651 010
Fax: (02) 6282 5810
IP Australia State Offices

The Institute of Patent and Trade Mark Attorneys
http://www.ipaustralia.gov.au/ip

2. Trade Marks

A trademark can be a letter, number, word, phrase, sound, smell, shape, logo, picture, aspect of packaging or any combination of these.

It is used to distinguish goods and services of one trade from those of another. This means you can't register a trademark that directly describes your goods (e.g. radios) and services (e.g. electrician).

While it is difficult to register a geographic name or surname, someone who has used one extensively in the marketplace for a considerable period of time may be able to achieve registration.

You don't have to register your trademark to use it.

However, registration is advisable because it can be an expensive and time consuming exercise to take action under common law. A registered trademark gives you the exclusive legal right to use, license or sell it within Australia for the goods and services for which it is registered.

Always search existing trademarks before using a mark or applying for registration. You may find yourself the subject of legal action if the mark you propose to use is already registered or in use by someone else.

ideas generation

Time limit
Initial registration of a trademark lasts for ten years. After that time you can continue to renew your registration for successive periods of ten years on payment of the appropriate fee.

A trademark can therefore have an infinite life representing significant business value. You must, however, use your mark in a bona fide way to avoid it becoming vulnerable to removal on the grounds of non-use.

Who administers trademarks?
Applications should be filed with the Trade Marks Office of IP Australia. They will examine your application to see if it meets legislative requirements.

Also, there is protection against misrepresentation under the trade practices or fair trading legislation and it is also possible to take action under common law.

Trade mark examples
- Qantas
- Poppy Lipsticks
- King Island
- Hound Dog Australia
- Uncle Tobys Super Series
- Redheads
- Deep Heat
- Chesty Bonds
- Tarzan's Grip

Useful addresses

IP Australian Head Office
PO Box 200
Woden ACT 2606
National Phone Number: 1300 651 010
Fax: (02) 6282 5810
Trade Marks Helpline: (02) 6283 2999
IP Australia State Offices

The Institute of Patent and Trade Mark Attorneys of Australia (IPTA)
1 Little Collins Street
Melbourne Vic 3000
Ph: (03) 9650 2399
Fax: (03) 9650 3511
Free call: 1800 804 536

Licensing Executive Society of Australia and New Zealand (LES)
PO Box 842
Mulgrave Vic 3170
Ph: (03) 9574 9651
Fax: (03) 9574 8066

The Australian Manufacturers of Patents, Industrial Designs, Copyright and Trade Mark Association (AMPICTA)
Level 12, 140 Arthur Street
North Sydney NSW 2060
Ph: (02) 9927 7500
Fax: (02) 9956 7004

ideas generation

3. Designs

Design refers to the features of shape, configuration, pattern or ornamentation which can be judged by the eye in finished articles.

Design registration is used to protect the visual appearance of manufactured products. To be registered, your design must be new or original.

A registered design gives you the exclusive and legally enforceable right to use, license or sell your design.

Note:

- Design registration is intended to protect designs which have an industrial or commercial use.
- Designs which are essentially ARTISTIC WORKS are covered by copyright legislation and ARE NOT ELIGIBLE for design registration.
- The protection you receive is only for the appearance of the article and not how it works.

Time limit

Initially, protection is for a period of 12 months but it can be extended for a total period of 16 years.

Who administers designs?

Applications should be filed with the Designs Office of IP Australia. They will assess whether your invention is new and if it meets the legislative requirements.

You can learn more about the patent process under the Designs section of this website.

Design examples
Electric Jug
Ken Done Bedlinen
Sebel Metal Frame Chair

A Folding Chair
A Dunlop Tyre
Speedo's
Canvas Chair
Metal Fencing
Portable Cooler
Squatters Chair
Tap Sealing
A Toy Building Block
A Rocking Kangaroo

Useful addresses
IP Australian Head Office
PO Box 200
Woden ACT 2606
National Phone Number: 1300 651 010
Fax: (02) 6282 5810
IP Australia State Offices

The Institute of Patent and Trade Mark Attorneys of Australia (IPTA)
1 Little Collins Street
Melbourne Vic 3000
Ph: (03) 9650 2399
Fax: (03) 9650 3511
Free call: 1800 804 536

Licensing Executive Society of Australia and New Zealand (LES)
PO Box 842
Mulgrave Vic 3170
Ph: (03) 9574 9651
Fax: (03) 9574 8066

ideas generation

The Australian Manufacturers of Patents, Industrial Designs, Copyright and Trade Mark Association (AMPICTA)
Level 12, 140 Arthur Street
North Sydney NSW 2060
Ph: (02) 9927 7500
Fax: (02) 9956 7004

4. Copyright

Copyright protects the original expression of ideas, not the ideas themselves. It is free and automatically safeguards your original works of art, literature, music, films, broadcasts and computer programs from copying and certain other uses.

Material is protected from the time it is first written down, painted or drawn, filmed or taped. Material may also enjoy reciprocal protection under the laws of other countries who are signatories to the Universal Copyright Convention.

Copyright protection is provided under the Copyright Act 1968 and gives exclusive rights to license others in regard to copying the work, performing it in public, broadcasting it, publishing it and making an adaptation of the work. Rights vary according to the nature of the work. Those for artistic works, for instance, are different from those for literary and musical works.

Although making copies of copyright material can infringe exclusive rights, a certain amount of copying is permissible under the fair dealing provisions of the legislation.

Copyright doesn't protect you against independent creation of a similar work. Legal actions against infringement are complicated by the fact that a number of different copyrights may exist in some works – particularly films, broadcasts and multimedia products.

Consider using a copyright notice
Although a copyright notice – with owner's name and date – is not necessary in Australia, it can help prove your ownership of the copyright, and is necessary to establish copyright overseas. It can also act as a deterrent to potential infringers.

Copyright is lost if the owner applies a three-dimensional artistic work industrially. In such a case, it is necessary to register the design if protection is required.

Time limit
This varies according to the nature of the work and whether or not it has been published.

Depending on the material, copyright for artistic and literary works generally lasts fify years from the year of the author's death or from the year of first publication.

Copyright for films and sound recordings lasts fifty years from their publication and for broadcasts, fifty years from the year in which they were made.

Who administers copyright?
The Attorney-General's Department administers the legislation for automatic rights to copyright.

Useful addresses
Information and Security Law Division, Intellectual Property Branch,
Attorney-General's Department
Robert Garran Offices
National Circuit
Barton ACT 2600
Ph: (02) 6250 6313
Fax: (02) 6250 5929
Internet: www.law.gov.au/copyright_enews/

ideas generation

The Australian Copyright Council
Suite 3, 245 Chalmers Street
Redfern NSW 2016
Ph: (02) 9318 1788
Fax: (02) 9698 3536
Internet: www.copyright.org.au

5. Circuit layout rights

Circuit layout rights automatically protect original layout designs for integrated circuits, and computer chips.

While these rights are based on copyright law principles they are a separate, unique form of protection.

There is no requirement for registration for the granting of rights to the owner of a layout design.

Circuit layouts are usually highly complex and the intellectual effort in creating an original layout may be considerable and of great value. An integrated circuit or chip made from the plans is the key to the operation of all kinds of electronic devices, from heart pacemakers to personal computers.

The owner of an original circuit layout has exclusive right to:

- copy the layout in a material form;
- make integrated circuits from the layout; and
- **exploit it commercially in Australia.**

Commercial exploitation may occur by importation, sale, hire or distribution of a layout or an integrated circuit made according to the layout.

Time limit

The maximum possible protection period is twenty years. Accordingly, rights in an original layout subsist for ten years – from the first commercial exploitation – provided this occurs within ten years from creation of the layout – or ten years from the year in which it was made, if not commercially exploited.

Who administers circuit layout rights?
The Attorney-General's Department administers the legislation for automatic rights to circuit layout rights.

Useful addresses
Information and Security Law Division, Intellectual Property Branch,
Attorney-General's Department
Robert Garran Offices, National Circuit
Barton ACT 2600
Ph: (02) 6250 6608
Fax: (02) 6250 5929
Internet: www.law.gov.au

6. Plant breeder's rights
Plant breeder's rights (PBR) are used to protect new varieties of plants by giving exclusive commercial rights to market a new variety or its reproductive material.

You can direct the production, sale and distribution of the new variety, receive royalties from the sale of plants or sell your rights.

Under eligibility provisions a new variety may be sold for up to twelve months in Australia, and four years overseas, and still remain eligible for plant breeder's rights.

To be eligible for protection you must:
- show that the new variety is distinct, as well as being uniform and stable;
- be able to demonstrate, by a comparative trial, that your variety is clearly distinguishable from any other variety, the existence of which is a matter of common knowledge.

ideas generation

Plant breeder's rights do not extend to the use of a grower's crop (that is, the grower does not have to pay a royalty on the crop produced), nor does it extend to the use of the variety in plant breeding or retention by growers of seed for the production of another crop on their land.

Time limit
Protection lasts for up to twenty-five years for trees or vines and 20 years for other species.

Who registers plant breeder's rights?
This is administered by Plant Breeder's Rights Australia in the Department of Agriculture, Fisheries and Forestry (AFFA). There is a registration and examination process. It's legally enforceable and gives exclusive commercial rights to a new plant variety.

Useful addresses
Plant Breeder's Rights Australia, Agriculture, Fisheries and Forestry Australia
GPO Box 858
Canberra ACT 2601
Ph: (02) 6272 4228
Fax: (02) 6272 3650
Internet: www.affa.gov.au/agfor/pbr/pbr.html

The Institute of Patent and Trade Mark Attorneys of Australia (IPTA)
1 Little Collins Street
Melbourne Vic 3000
Ph: (03) 9650 2399
Fax: (03) 9650 3511
Free call: 1800 804 536

Licensing Executive Society of Australia and New Zealand (LES)
PO Box 842
Mulgrave Vic 3170
Ph: (03) 9574 9651
Fax: (03) 9574 8066

The Australian Manufacturers of Patents, Industrial Designs, Copyright and Trade Mark Association (AMPICTA)
Level 12, 140 Arthur Street
North Sydney NSW 2060
Ph: (02) 9927 7500
Fax: (02) 9956 7004

7. Trade secrets

A trade secret is both a type of IP and a strategy for protecting your IP. It can provide effective protection for some technologies, proprietary knowledge (know-how), confidential information and other forms of IP.

A confidentiality agreement is often used to stop employees from revealing your secret or proprietary knowledge during and after their employment or association with your business.

- **Make sure you back up your trade secret with signed confidentiality agreements with every person who has knowledge of the secret.**

If an agreement is breached, you will have evidence of what was agreed and protection through the law.

When is a trade secret strategy appropriate?

Perhaps your IP is unlikely to result in a registrable right, or maybe you want to retain exclusive use beyond the term of a patent.

A trade secret strategy is appropriate when it's difficult

ideas generation

to copy the construction, manufacturing process or formulation from the product itself – that is, when reverse engineering is unlikely.

Be aware. Secrecy does not stop anyone else from inventing the same product or process independently and exploiting it commercially. It does not give you exclusive rights and you are vulnerable when employees with this knowledge leave your firm.

Trade secrets are difficult to maintain over longer periods or when a larger number of people are made privy to the secret.

Proving a breach of confidentiality under common law can be complex and is potentially more costly than defending registered rights.

- Ask contractors and employees to provide written undertakings not to compete with your business after they leave in, addition to signing a confidentiality agreement. It is often much easier to prove this than to prove breach of confidentiality. These undertakings, however, are difficult to enforce and need to be prepared by your legal adviser, as you need to be careful that the undertaking does not restrict the contractor's or employee's right to earn a living.

What if someone infringes my trade secret?
Common law provides protection for infringement of trade secrets, breach of confidentiality agreements and passing off trade marks.

Business, company and domain names
Know the difference! Choosing the right name for your new business, company or selecting an Internet domain name is vital to distinguish your goods and services from

competitors. You are creating an identity-something memorable and meaningful.

Business, company names and domain names are best protected when they are registered as trade marks. If your new name is identical or similar to another person's registered trade mark, you could be sued for infringement. Commercial names can be trade marks, business names, company names and domain names. This can be very confusing so it's important to know the difference.

What is a business name?
A business name is the name under which a business operates, and registration identifies the owners of that business. Registration is compulsory, in every state and territory from which a business operates, and must be completed before the business starts trading. Unlike trade marks, business names do not necessarily provide proprietary rights for the use of the trading name.

What is a company name?
A company name, or registrable body, must be registered with the Australian Securities and Investment Commission. If a company wishes to trade using a name other than its registered company name, it must register that trading name as a business name. Unlike trade marks, company names do not necessarily provide proprietary rights for the use of the trading name.

What is a domain name?
All computers on the Internet have a unique identifying number called an Internet Protocol address. The Internet Protocol address is what a computer uses to find an Internet site. Unfortunately, it is not intuitive or easy for

people to remember. A domain name is the unique name that corresponds with an Internet Protocol address. It is both intuitive and easy to remember.

In Australia, you cannot register your trade mark as a domain name unless the trade mark is the same as your legal entity name (i.e. business or company name). The rules and policies for registration of domain names in com.au may be viewed at http://www.internet-namesww.com.au/.

You can also register a domain name as a trade mark, provided that it meets the requirements of the Trade Marks Act.

Registration of a business, company or domain name does not automatically give you the right to use that name as a trade mark. You should check the trade marks database before registering a business name, company name or domain name in order to avoid infringing someone else's trade mark.

Who administers business, company and domain names?
Business names are administered by the local Business Names office in your State or Territory.

The Australian Securities and Investments Commission is responsible for the administration of company names. They have Business Centres in Adelaide, Brisbane, Canberra, Geelong, Gold Coast, Hobart, Melbourne, Newcastle, Perth, Sydney and Townsville.

Internet Names WorldWide governs the registration of com.au domain names. On the Internet, 'com' stands for a commercial site and 'au' is the country code for Australia.

INA was one of the first domain name authorities in the world to undertake mandatory searches on company name, business name and trade mark databases for possible infringements before domain name registration can proceed.

Useful addresses
Business Names:
Contact the Business Names Office in your State or Territory

Company Names:
Contact Australian Securities and Investments Commission Business Centre (ASIC)
Adelaide, Brisbane, Canberra, Geelong, Gold Coast, Hobart, Melbourne, Newcastle, Perth, Sydney, Townsville
Internet: www.asic.gov.au

Domain Names:
Internet Names WorldWide
Level 3, 207 Bouverie Street
Carlton Vic 3053
Ph: 1800 354 595 or (03) 9344 9366
Fax: (03) 9349 4267
Internet: www.internetnamesww.com.au

IP Australia National Office
PO Box 200
Woden ACT 2606
Fax: (02) 6282 5810
National phone number: 1300 651 010
Trade Marks Helpline: (02) 6283 2999
IP Australia State Offices

ideas generation

Ownership of IP rights

Creating IP does not mean you own the rights to it! With the exception of copyright and circuit layout rights, which are automatic, you must take formal steps to register your IP and obtain the legal rights of ownership. Otherwise, you will have to rely on common law to prove ownership and prior use for non-registered IP.

Gain and maintain the rights to your IP. Ownership of IP rights is the legal recognition you receive for your creative effort. It gives you the right to fully exploit your IP – to own, sell, license or bequeath your IP in much the same way as you can with real estate.

Having the ability to assign or license those rights allows you maximum flexibility in choosing a course of action that will best profit your business.

Copyright and circuit layout rights are automatically granted upon creation. You must register all other IP rights with the relevant government organisation.

If you don't develop appropriate strategies to protect your IP from an early stage, you may lose your legal right to patent your innovative product or idea.

If you tell someone about your ideas before seeking appropriate protection, or sell unpatented products, your competitors can use them.

Your products will no longer be considered new so you will be unable to obtain a patent. Nor will you be able to protect your products from being copied.

Some types of IP rights need to be maintained, e.g. by paying annual maintenance fees, in order to keep your legal right to use the IP exclusively. Different IP rights vary in the protection they provide. Often, more than one may be necessary to fully protect your creation.

Note: Registering your IP rights in Australia does not give you international protection. You must apply for this separately.

International protection
Protect your overseas markets. You need to seek IP protection in each country according to the laws and conventions of that country, although there are international agreements in place which make it easier to obtain rights in other countries.

International agreements
International IP Agreements to which Australia is a party:
- Convention Establishing the World Intellectual Property Organization (WIPO)
- Trans-Tasman Mutual Recognition Agreement for the Patent Attorney Profession
- Paris Convention for the Protection of Industrial Property
- Patent Cooperation Treaty (PCT)
- Strasbourg Agreement Concerning the International Patent Classification
- Nice Agreement for the International Classification of Goods and Services for the Purposes of the Registration of Marks
- World Trade Organisation Agreement on Trade-Related Aspects of Intellectual Property Rights (TRIPS)
- Budapest Treaty on the International Recognition of the Deposit of Microorganisms for the Purposes of Patent Procedure

Convention Establishing the World Intellectual Property Organization (WIPO)

WIPO is an intergovernmental organisation with headquarters in Geneva and is one of the sixteen United Nations specialised agencies. WIPO is responsible for promoting intellectual property throughout the world through cooperation among member states and for the administration of various unions, each founded by a multilateral treaty and dealing with the legal and administrative aspects of intellectual property.

WIPO was established in 1970, but its origins go back to 1883 and 1886 with the Paris and Berne Conventions. On 1 January 1997, there were 161 members.

Australia has been a member of WIPO since August 1972 and was a member of its predecessor, the United International Bureau for the Protection of Intellectual Property (BIRPI).

Trans-Tasman Mutual Recognition Agreement for the Patent Attorney Profession

The Trans-Tasman Mutual Recognition Agreement between the Government of Australia and the Government of New Zealand came into operation on 1 May 1998.

The purpose of the Agreement and the enabling laws is to give effect to the two mutual recognition principles relating to the sale of goods and the registration of occupations, consistent with the protection of public health and safety and the environment.

The mutual recognition principles are:
- if goods may legally be sold in New Zealand, they may legally be sold in an Australian jurisdiction and visa versa; and

- if a person is registered to practice an occupation in New Zealand, he or she will be entitled to practice an equivalent occupation in an Australian jurisdiction and visa versa.

The legislation:
- provides that, where there is a requirement for registration to practise and where there is an equivalent occupation in the other jurisdiction, a person will have the right to apply for registration in that jurisdiction provided they are registered in the original jurisdiction.
- waives many of the requirements for registration with the sole determinant being 'equivalence of occupation'.
- applies to registered patent attorneys in Australia and New Zealand with the consequence that registered patent attorneys in both countries will have the right to apply for registration in the other jurisdiction from 1 May 1998.

IP Australia and the Intellectual Property Office of New Zealand have agreed on procedures to facilitate registration in either jurisdiction.

Applicants for registration will be required to complete an application and submit it, together with the appropriate fees, to the relevant registration authority. All fees are payable in the currency of the relevant registering authority.

Further information can be obtained from:

Australia:
Secretary, Professional Standards Board for Patent and Trade Marks Attorneys, Phone: + 61 2 6283 2345
New Zealand:
Manager, Intellectual Property Office of New Zealand,
Phone: +64 4 560 1613

Paris Convention for the Protection of Industrial Property

The Paris Convention is concerned with the protection of industrial property, which includes patents, industrial designs and trade marks, and with the repression of unfair competition.

In a key provision the convention requires each member country to accord nationals of other member countries the same rights for their industrial property as it accords to its own nationals. It provides a right of priority for applicants for patents, trade marks and designs in any of the member countries deriving from the date of the first application for the invention, trade mark or design concerned in any other member country, provided the subsequent applications are made within a prescribed period after the first application.

The convention does not seek to establish a uniform international industrial property system as such, but rather to establish an international framework upon which the national laws of its member countries can be built. The convention is currently the subject of negotiations relating to a proposed revision to help the transfer of patented technology to developing countries.

On 1 January 1997, there were 140 members of the Paris Convention. Australia has been a member since October 1925.

Patent Cooperation Treaty (PCT)

The Patent Cooperation Treaty provides a unified system through which to apply for patent protection in member countries. The PCT permits the filing of a single international application in a member country to have the effect of a national filing in each of the 89 member countries designated by the applicant.

The international application is subjected to a mandatory international search and may undergo an international preliminary examination before each designated country determines under its national laws whether to grant or refuse a patent.

Australia has been a member of the PCT since March 1980. The Australian Patent Office acts as a receiving office, international searching authority and international preliminary examining authority under the PCT.

Budapest Treaty on the International Recognition of the Deposit of Microorganisms for the Purposes of Patent Procedure

The Budapest Treaty provides for the deposit of microorganisms in an international depositary authority (IDA) where a deposit is necessary to satisfy the descriptive requirements of patents legislation for inventions involving a microorganism or the use of a microorganism. The deposit assures access to the microorganism by persons other than the inventor for the purposes of testing or experimenting, or for commercial use when the patent expires.

Under the treaty a member State which allows or requires the deposit of microorganisms for the purposes of patent procedure must recognise, for such purposes, one deposit of a microorganism with any IDA, irrespective of its location.

On 1 January 1997, there were thirty-eight members of the Budapest Treaty. Australia has been a member since July 1987. The Australian Government Analytical Laboratories acquired the status of an IDA in September 1988.

Strasbourg Agreement Concerning the International Patent Classification

The Strasbourg Agreement established an international system for the classification of patent documents to identify noteworthy technical content. The purpose behind the agreement is to replace the individual classification systems of national patent offices by a uniform classification system for patent documents of all member countries, thus facilitating information retrieval and international comparisons.

On 1 January 1997, there were thirty-eight members of the Strasbourg Agreement. Australia became party to the agreement in November 1975. The International Patent Classification (IPC) has been the sole classification system used for Australian patent documents since 1976.

Nice Agreement for the International Classification of Goods and Services for the Purposes of the Registration of Marks

The Nice Agreement established a classification which consists of a list of thirty-four classes for marks which are applied to goods and eight classes for marks which relate to services. There is also an alphabetical list of goods and services comprising approximately 11,000 items.

On 1 January 1997, there were fifty members of the Nice Agreement. Australia became a member in April 1961 and uses the classification of goods and services which has been developed under the Nice Agreement.

World Trade Organisation Agreement on Trade-Related Aspects of Intellectual Property Rights (TRIPS)

The TRIPS Agreement provides minimum standards of IP protection with members being free to determine the appropriate method of implementing the provisions of the Agreement within their own legal system and practice.

As is usual in IP conventions, TRIPS contains national treatment provisions, under which the nationals of other members must be given treatment no less favourable than that accorded to members' own nationals with regard to intellectual property protection.

There is also a Most-Favoured-Nation (MFN) provision – a first in an IP convention. Under this provision, with certain well-established exceptions, any advantage or benefit a member gives to the nationals of another member country must be extended immediately and unconditionally to the nationals of all other members – even if this treatment is more favourable than that which it accords to its own nationals.

The TRIPS Agreement also includes provisions for the prevention and settlement of disputes in respect of the implementation of its provisions.

On 28 April 1997 there were 131 members of the World Trade Organisation. Developing member states have until 1 January 2000 to implement the provisions of the Agreement and least developed countries in 2006. Australia became party to this Agreement on 1 January 1995 when it first came into force.

This is a costly process, particularly when it involves the translation of applications into other languages.

You may be eligible for government assistance to help meet the costs of international protection for overseas markets, under Austrade's Export Market Development Grant Scheme.

Seek advice before you publish or use your IP.

ideas generation

Once you apply for protection in one country, you may apply for protection in other member countries under international conventions, providing it is within the following time limits:
- patents and plant breeder's rights: twelve months from the date of the first application in a member country;
- designs and trade marks: six months from the date of the first application in a member country.

This gives you the opportunity to obtain exclusive rights to your IP in overseas markets. Your applications in those countries will have a 'priority date', which is the filing date of your original application.

While you can apply outside these time limits, you cannot obtain the benefit of the international convention and any earlier disclosure of your invention or design may invalidate your rights in those countries.

Please note that some countries are not members of the convention and any publication or use of your IP can prevent you obtaining protection in those countries.

International IP professionals
AWA Patent (Sweden)
Baker and McKenzie (59 offices worldwide)
Baldwin Shelston Waters (Auckland, Wellington, Christchurch)
Blake Dawson Waldron (London, Port Moresby, Jakarta, Shanghai, Hong Kong)
Chartered Institute of Patent Agents (UK)
Coudert Brothers (27 Offices Worldwide)
Freehill Hollingdale & Page (Hanoi, Ho Chi Minh City, Jakarta)
Institute of Professional Representatives before the European Patent Office (EPI)

F.R. Kelly & Co. (Dublin, Ireland)
Mallesons Stephen Jaques (Hong Kong, Beijing, Taipei, Jakarta, Port Moresby and London)
Minter Ellison (Hong Kong, Singapore, Jakarta, London, New York, New Zealand)
A.J. Park and Son (Auckland and Wellington, New Zealand)
Pharaon and Partners (Jordan)
Phillips Fox Lawyers (Auckland, Wellington, Hanoi, Ho Chi Minh City)
James W. Piper & Co (Auckland, New Zealand)
Wilson Gunn M'Caw (Manchester, England)
Validia Patent Group (Minsk, Belarus)

Search firms
Brands and Logos International (Trade Mark Search and Information Service)
Platonic Hood Patents Online (Patent, Trade Mark and Design Search Service)
R.E Kemp & Co Pty Limited (Patent, Trade Mark and Design Search Service)

Developing Strategies To Protect Your IP Rights

Today, you developed an idea that will revolutionise the world...

Who will be reaping the rewards of your innovation – you or someone else?

Global markets are becoming increasingly aggressive. Everyone is searching for that competitive edge – that special something that will make you stand out from the rest.

IP often provides the leverage needed for successful companies to stay ahead of the pack. That makes

ideas generation

protecting your IP essential. After all, the only one who should benefit from your innovation is you, right?!

Building effective strategies around your IP will give your business a major, sustainable market advantage. IP is as important to commercial success as business, marketing and financial plans. Smart businesses place their IP alongside other assets on the company balance sheet.

Don't put yourself at risk!
Do not forfeit ownership of your IP rights, in Australia or in potential overseas markets, through hasty, ill-informed decisions. Do not talk about your idea or make it public too soon, or you may lose the legal right to exclusive use of your IP.

IP ownership gives you an extremely valuable asset – it may be the most effective business tool you will ever use!

Well, that's really what we're talking about here, isn't it?! Creating it, increasing it, keeping it.

Learn from the experiences of others who have already gone down the road. Fail to do so and you may put your business at risk. Do not talk about your idea or make it public too soon, or you may lose the legal right to exclusive use of your IP.

Make sure that, when disclosing or marketing your invention or design in Australia, you do not invalidate a future patent or design in another country.

Different IP rights vary in the protection they provide. Often, more than one type may be necessary to fully protect your creation.

Finding the right lawyer
There are a number of lawyers who can act as your legal counsel. Before you settle on one, you should ' interview'

three or four potential candidates. Who you choose depends largely on the funds you can dedicate to legal fees and the size of your ideas team.

If you are going it alone, then it is probably better for you to find a smaller law firm that is happy to handle you and give you some real attention. The last thing you want to do is go to the biggest intellectual property law firm and end up paying top dollar for not much at all.

This is not to say that all large firms treat the small clients in this way, but it is unusual for an individual to retain a large firm. You need to find a firm that understands you, is willing to listen, might be interested in taking a percentage of the equity rather than an upfront fee and will treat you in a professional manner.

Do some desk research, use the Internet or go to some of the Web sites we have recommended and shop around.

Non-disclosure Agreements (NDA) and Confidentiality Agreements

A non-disclosure agreement (sometimes called a confidentiality agreement) is an agreement between two parties not allowing either to disclose information of conversations or dealings with a third party.

This type of document is something that every ideas generator should almost carry with them in their back pocket. Although it doesn't guarantee that the party you are dealing with will not 'let something slip' to a third party, it still gives the discussions some level of formality and commitment. It can act as a little extra deterrent to stop the other party from speaking to somebody else.

ideas generation

NDAs are relatively straightforward documents and there are numerous Web sites you can access to download a template.

Check out:
ideasgeneration.com.au
viausa.com/NonDisclosure
trisignal.com/nda
goldtree.com/links/Library/Non_Disclosure_Agreement

This is a standard practice. Do not feel afraid to ask all the individuals you come in contact with to sign an NDA. It is unlikely that a professional will resist.

11

The Road Ahead

A final thought. Five things to remember.

A final thought

There are some who believe that in business, as in life, nature must (and will) take its course. If you have done everything in your power to get your idea up and running and for some reason it falls over at the eleventh hour, maybe it just wasn't meant to be.

Sometimes nature has its own timetable. Serendipity plays its own role and sometimes no matter what you do, you cannot force something into being.

Wise men say that if you chase the God of Knowledge, the God of Wealth will follow.

If you love what you do and have a passion for generating ideas, the rest will follow.

Ideas generators, we salute you!

Five things to remember

If you would like to, photocopy the following page and stick it in your diary or on your fridge. It will become the one page you need that will keep you generating ideas. We call it the five things to remember page.

ideas generation

Thing to Remember Number 1:
Everyone is creative – we are all born that way. Never let anybody tell you that you are unable to be an ideas generator. No one can ever corner the market on creativity or new ideas. Why? Because ideas are about originality and we are all capable of that.

Thing to Remember Number 2:
Ideas are like cancer. Get the ideas you have out of your head and into the world. Don't let them fester. Let them live and breathe on their own. Do whatever it takes to get them down on paper. Keep going back to the 21 Ideas Step Production Line.

Thing to Remember Number 3:
Volume. You need to come up with one hundred ideas before you have one that is good enough to make it to the marketplace. This means you should never become too attached to your ideas. We said this before and we will say it again: Ideas are a dime a dozen. Do not lose your perspective so that you are unable to see whether your idea has any real shot in the world.

Thing to Remember Number 4:
Keep your mouth closed! Do not tell anybody about your idea. If you speak about it to someone, you have to assume that they will steal it if it is any good. The possibility of vast sums of money does strange things to people. Stealing a good idea is the oldest trick in the business world. Many people have become rich on the back of somebody else's great idea.

Thing to Remember Number 5:
Get legal counsel before you start negotiations. As we have said before, you have done your job, now let your legal counsel do theirs. Do not think that you can negotiate anything yourself. A good lawyer is worth every cent.